The Circulating Swing, a Treatment for Insanity, 1818

WHO

REDISCOVERING COMMUNITY

CARES?

DAVID B. SCHWARTZ

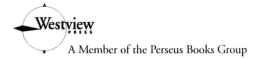

Westview
PRESS

A Member of the Perseus Books Group

Copyright © 1997 by **Westview Press, A Member of the Perseus Books Group**

Published in 1997 in the United States of America by Westview Press, 5500 Central Avenue, Boulder, Colorado 80301-2877, and in the United Kingdom by Westview Press, 12 Hid's Copse Road, Cumnor Hill, Oxford OX2 9JJ

Library of Congress Cataloging-in-Publication Data
Schwartz, David B., 1948–
  Who cares? : rediscovering community / David B. Schwartz.
    p.   cm.
  Includes bibliographical references and index.
  ISBN 0-8133-3207-9 (hc). — ISBN 0-8133-3208-7 (pb)
    1. Handicapped—Care.   2. Caregivers.   3. Community.   I. Title.
HV1568.S38   1997
362.4—dc20   96-34625
                                                                                                              CIP

The paper used in this publication meets the requirements of the American Standard for Permanence of Paper for Printed Library Materials Z39.48-1984.

10   9

TO LEE HOINACKI AND
SEYMOUR B. SARASON

Suppose, again, that the other endured labour and weariness in teaching me; that, besides the ordinary sayings of teachers, there are things which he has transmitted and instilled into me; that by his encouragement he aroused the best that was in me, at one time inspirited me by his praise, at another warned me to put aside sloth; that, laying hand, so to speak, on my mental powers that then were hidden and inert, he drew them forth into the light; that, instead of doling out his knowledge grudgingly in order that there might be the longer need of his service, he was eager, if he could, to pour the whole of it into me—if I do not owe to such a man all the love that I give to those to whom I am bound by the most grateful ties, I am indeed ungrateful.

—Seneca

The triumph of the industrial economy is the fall of community. But the fall of community reveals how precious and how necessary community is. For when community falls, so must fall all the things that only community life can engender and protect: the care of the old, the care and education of children, family life, neighborly work, the handing down of memory, the care of the earth, respect for nature and the lives of wild creatures.

—Wendell Berry

Nobody would choose to live without friends even if he had all the other good things.

—Aristotle

CONTENTS

FIGURES

FOREWORD

When David Schwartz finished the manuscript for this book, he invited me to Harrisburg. I arrived, and we met at a sidewalk café, a pleasant adornment to the not quite matching but nicely maintained row houses in the shadow of the robber baron State Capitol. Schwartz was at the end of a month's vacation. He had spent a lot of time sitting at his usual table at the North Street Café, touching people's lives. This sometimes resulted in a certain match between two people—for example, a woman in a wheelchair with a shy and lonely but generous computer operator; a bright, twelve-year-old dyslexic boy with a palsied bachelor lawyer. Each had something to give the other.

Schwartz the man fits in no category. He has nothing of the meddler; rather, he possesses an unusual eye for the unexpected havens of sanity through which people respond to each other. He is not a do-gooder; when he invites two people to reach out to one another, he has no vision of the outcome. He does not fall into the role of matchmaker or gossip; he challenges those who meet through him to let themselves be surprised. His wit and dry humor have helped protect him from a pitfall of social service professionals; he has recovered from well-intentioned reforms that channel clients into mimicries of neighborhood, thereby confirming their inmate status.

With painful clear-sightedness, Schwartz has seen two things: what professional diagnosis, therapy, and institutional care do to the handicapped and, more important, the degree to which ritual segregation and treatment cement society's negative expectations about them. He does not repeat but rather complements the work of his predecessors John McKnight, Jerome Miller, and Nils Christie. Further, in one very important way Schwartz goes beyond them: He shows how these negative expectations are the main reason for an endemic blindness to the widespread readiness of ordinary people to provide individual handicapped persons with lifelong hospitality.

Ivan Illich

CREDITS

Grateful acknowledgment is made to the following for permission to quote or to reproduce figures:

WHO CARES?

INTRODUCTION

When I was a boy, I sometimes used to go along in the truck with my Uncle Erwin to fix big refrigeration systems. I got to carry his toolbox, in which his wrenches and gauges were laid out in precise order. We would climb way up into the attic of some movie theater to the place where massive air-conditioning machinery whirred to find out what was broken.

Uncle Erwin always did the same thing: He crouched down on his haunches in front of some big, complicated unit bristling with pipes and hoses and wires and ducts and motors and fanbelts, and he listened. He would cock his head from side to side and listen to all of the different noises. Sometimes he wrinkled his nose and sniffed for overheated oil or a slight electrical burning odor. After a long time, during which I was squirming, anxiously waiting to break out the tools and tear that big thing apart looking for the problem, he would get up. He'd walk over to some of the pipes and put one rough hand around the cold pipe and one around the warm return, and he'd look off reflectively into space. His reverie, I believe, concerned physics. Refrigeration works by the way liquids, turning to their gaseous state, transfer energy as heat. With one hand on a copper pipe full of hot gas and the other on one filled with cold liquid, he was assessing the dynamic physical chemistry of the system.

I was *really* ready to break out the tools by now. But not my uncle. He would sit down on his haunches again, pull his keys out of his pocket, clean his ear with a key, and squint at the huge piece of equipment in front of him. After what seemed to me an interminable wait, he'd get up, look over at me, and say, "Hand me a 3/8-inch socket with the long extender, would you?" With that wrench he would reach into the bowels of the cooling unit and instantly fix what was wrong.

With my Uncle Erwin there was never any thrashing around, digging for the problem, tearing machinery to pieces, with parts scattered around his feet. By the time he picked up a tool, he knew exactly what needed to be done. As a boy I watched him work, and it made a deep impression on me.

1

When I was a little older, my father started taking me along with him on speaking trips. My job was to show the slides. I sat in the projection booth of some dental school auditorium, and I showed slides of patients from his clinic in various stages of treatment for temporomandibular joint disorders. The typical patient would come to him after undergoing major surgery or radical grinding of teeth and adjustment of bite, only to find himself or herself in even more pain. My father emphasized conservative practice: slow, minor changes over time, reassurance, physical therapy, even psychotherapy in many situations.

He emphasized one thing most of all, and I heard it over and over again from the back of the hall. "Conduct a careful history!" he would command. "Sit the new patient down in your office—far out of sight of all of that intimidating dental equipment—and ask him or her what has happened. *Listen* to him or her. *Only* when you have a thorough understanding of what the difficulty might be should you even *consider* picking up your rapidly rotating dental tools!" As a young man I listened, and his words also made a deep impression on me.

I followed neither my uncle nor my father into their respective fields. For most of my adult life I have been involved in the field of disabilities: establishing programs and directing public policy. Over many years of such work, I have increasingly come to realize that social programs are often established, and influential social policy is frequently made, with far less reflection than my uncle used to fix an air conditioner.

Despite constant efforts to erect new caring systems and to reform old ones, it is beginning to come to general awareness that our systematized approach to caring for vulnerable people is suffering from widespread failure. I have come to believe that our persistence in pursuing counterproductive ways of seeing the need for care and arranging for its provision can be traced to certain interrelated assumptions that we do not ordinarily question or examine.

In all enterprises, understanding the complexity of what you are attempting to do is at least as important as taking decisive action. As my father said, you have to take a history. Thus I attempt in this book to penetrate something of the complex phenomenon of modern care, to delineate the assumptions beneath such care, and to trace what might be learned from history about the formation of these assumptions.

The way we think about caring is not a theoretical but a practical question for me. Setting up programs to care for people has been my work. In this work I have been trying to learn from my first two important teachers, my father and my uncle. I want to approach the body of society with at least as much reflection as my uncle approached a refrigerator or my father a patient in pain. Such reflection may be worthwhile before one picks up the blunt tools of social policy: money, programs, and laws.

In this book I compare two different ways of approaching caring: a formal, systemic way and an informal way. I examine the fairly different kinds of relationships between people that characterize each approach and look into the different ways they originated and their differing consequences. I ask why the formal idea has become so dominant that informal approaches have become rather neglected. I examine some of the consequences of this dominance and explore the possibility of alternatives.

In Chapter 1 I delineate the formal and informal ideas. In the second chapter I examine the consequences of the dominance of the formal idea in caring. Chapter 3 takes up the issue of the dynamics that help to maintain this dominance through economics and language. How does an uncontrolled expansion of formal systems devour the informal? The fourth chapter makes a case that in a world dominated by formal structures, a generalized yearning for a sense of community, which is so much a characteristic of modern life, appears as a predictable indicator of that which has been displaced and lost.

How did caring, which originally existed only as an informal phenomenon I term *hospitality*, become the systematized industry it is today? In the fifth chapter I draw upon the work of social historian and philosopher Ivan Illich to explore his historical theses suggesting how this took place. I take up in Chapter 6 a search for remnants of informal hospitality in the modern systemic world, using as an example the neighborhood in which I live. Can informal impulses for hospitality in society be stimulated? If so, might care result? In Chapter 7 I look at the work of some practical social visionaries, among them a psychiatrist and two physicians, to see how they accomplished such stimulation.

By Chapter 8 the reader may have gained the impression that I dismiss the possibilities for hospitality and caring within formal structures. I here take the opportunity to correct this, looking at the conditions in which exemplary caring and hospitality continue to exist as informal traditions within formal institutions. Chapter 9 examines three factors that help maintain a continuing emphasis on formal approaches: current public policies, an unbalanced emphasis on individual rights, and the socialization of professionals.

In Chapter 10 I take up commonly proposed solutions to the problems noted, with particular reference to the political debate of the mid-1990s, and say why I don't think they will work. In Chapter 11 I ask what possibilities exist for taking a different approach to social healing and hospitality that recognize the importance of informal cultural life, and I summarize the kinds of actions I believe can help. In the final chapter I take up the inevitable question—so what can one do?—answering this in a personal fashion. I also raise one final question—can community be understood as a social phenonemon, or is it necessarily a transcendent question anchored in a specific place?

In this book I have drawn heavily upon the work of Ivan Illich, so much so that it is impractical to cite each individual instance in which I have been influenced by his thought. Suffice it to say that my work here is so permeated with his thinking that many insights the reader might take to be mine are certainly his. This is especially true in Chapters 3, 4, and 5, the last of which attempts to summarize Illich's views on the history of hospitality. I have spent much of the last several years attempting to comprehend Illich's work and to test it on the hard rock of practical experience in the making of public policy. I am deeply indebted to him for his interest, friendship, and hospitality offered in the various places where he has pitched his tents.

I owe a considerable debt of appreciation to a number of other individuals, of whom I can mention only a few. Seymour Sarason encouraged me to undertake this project, held my feet to the fire in clarifying my approach, and helped greatly in my research and preparation of the final text. Lee Hoinacki led me through the complexity of Illich's thinking, which would have been infinitely more difficult to decipher alone. He also assisted with a careful edit of the text that was, in itself, a tutorial in philosophical analysis and composition. This project was an excuse for spending many delightful hours together. Ross Speck of the Union Institute served as a tremendously helpful and supportive adviser and guide, as did Anne Wallace-DiGarbo and Janice Meier. I am deeply appreciative to all of these friends for the help and sacrifices they made to help me complete this project. I am grateful for important conversations with such other friends as Bob Duggan, John McKnight, and the late Christian Marzahn, which did much to shape my thinking. In addition, I wish to thank the chairperson, Joe Leonard, and members of the Pennsylvania Developmental Disabilities Planning Council, of which I served as director from 1983 to 1996. They are an example of a rare group of people who are as deeply committed to reflection before action as they are to effecting social improvement. I am indebted to Michelle Baxter of Westview Press for keen editorial advice in the revision of the final text. Finally, Marcus Schwartz's and Jim Stutzman's help with illustrations was invaluable, and, as always, I have deeply benefited from the editorial assistance and advice of my wife, Beth.

If I have learned anything in the writing of this book, it is that it has illuminated for me, much more than before, the possibilities of friendship and the unexpected adventures that may arise from this most cherished part of life and work.

David B. Schwartz

one

TWO WORLDS OF CARING

When my friend Gerald looked out his office window, he saw the woman about to jump off the bridge. She stood on the edge, wavering. Below her the Susquehanna River flowed rapidly around the bridge footings, carrying flood logs and debris over the dam and to the Chesapeake Bay. Behind her, busy traffic sped home from work to the West Shore, drivers and passengers listening to traffic reports on the radio.

Gerald stood for a minute, frozen. What should he do? He seemed to be the only person who had spotted the woman, from his vantage point one story above the street. Shaking himself into movement, he grabbed the telephone and started to dial the emergency number 911. Could the police and the ambulance and the crisis intervention team possibly make it there in time? What would the woman do when she heard the police sirens speeding to her rescue?

As his fingers punched the numbers, he saw a city bus rounding the turn onto the bridge. The bus drove slowly along the edge of the right lane. As it neared the woman, he saw the front accordian door open. Then suddenly—almost too fast to see if his eyes hadn't been riveted on the scene—the driver, in one continuous motion, stopped, leaned out of the open door, grabbed the woman's arm from behind, and pulled her backward into his bus.

My friend sat down, shaking slightly, and replaced the telephone receiver in its cradle. He thought about what he'd seen. And because he was a reflective person, he thought about what he had done. As he explained to me later, he realized that his response to the life-or-death situation of this stranger, this woman, had been to mobilize the complex human services system set up and ready to deal with such situations. That is what anyone would do, would they not? But the bus driver had responded completely differently. He had not flagged down a police officer. He had not dialed 911. He had seen the situation and had immediately done something himself. He had grabbed the woman by the arm and pulled her into his bus. Why, Gerald asked himself, had he not dashed down the stairs and across the street and done that very thing?

This book is about that question. Specifically, it is about two different ways that we, as individuals and as a society, have of responding to the situations of people who appear to be in need. They represent two different ways of living. One approach has to do with the formal world of systemic ways to help people. The other has to do with the informal world of personal responses people may make from within the context of historical traditions and out of some degree of personal autonomy. The first, in this instance, was Gerald's. The second was the bus driver's.

Why do some individuals act like the bus driver, whereas others do not? What is there about contemporary living that makes it more likely that one will respond like Gerald than like the bus driver? Finally, how might we go about explaining this characteristic of modern existence historically? These questions, too, are part of the subject of this book.

One of the certainties of modern existence is that we respond to the situation of people who are ill or hungry or dying or about to jump off a bridge by erecting and maintaining complex professional human service systems. By "certainty" Ivan Illich means something—an idea—that is so deeply ingrained in current shared perception and thought that the "rightness" of it is as sure as the ground beneath one's feet. Gerald's reach for the telephone is a good example of how this particular certainty forms the ground for our response, our consideration of the scope of possibilities for action, for this kind of situation. I recognize it as a certainty because had I been in Gerald's office, I would have done exactly the same thing.

Taking up Illich's investigations, I would like to consider how this belief has arisen, why we have become so certain that the best or perhaps even the sole way to respond to people is through the development of professional service systems, and some of the consequences of this belief. And I would like to examine the possibilities for action like that of the bus driver's that may yet exist outside of the formal systemic sphere.

Dying in the Arms of Your Friends

Questions like these might be thought of as "merely" theoretical, but they are of practical interest to me. For many years I worked as a public official in state government, directing the activities of a state council. The council's charge was to try to improve the lives of people within a certain administrative category of disabilities, called "developmental," in our commonwealth. This label includes people with mental retardation, cerebral palsy, autism, and related disabilities. Since we were concerned about these people, we were also interested in their families, their neighborhoods, their communities, and the interrelationship of these groups with each other. Since the council's job was to give out grants to stimulate new approaches to improving the lives of such people, an understanding of what approaches actually may or may not improve things was of concrete importance in determining what to do and how to spend the public money entrusted to its charge.

My former organization funds many efforts to improve professional systems and services. But a large interest of the council's, and particularly of mine, has had to do with discovering whether the inclination of ordinary people to help—like that of the bus driver—can be recognized and nurtured. Is it reasonable to expect that people in communities can take care of each other? The council's adventures in finding out whether this is so were the subject of a previous book of mine: *Crossing the River: Creating a Conceptual Revolution in Community and Disability.*[1]

One of the main things we learned from the experiments described in the earlier book was that ordinary citizens *will help people with disabilities if they are asked to do so.* We sponsored the work of people in certain communities whose job it was to ask others to become involved in the life of a specific person. I began to refer to these people as "askers." One of these askers became involved in the life of a woman named Nancy Lee.

Nancy was a woman with severe cerebral palsy who had spent a good part of her almost forty years of life in a nursing home. It was a miserable, gray, institutional place, but Nancy and many others like her had no place else to go. Initially she had grown up with her family, but after a while it had become impossible for them to do all of the constant work necessary for Nancy to live at home. Today in our state there is a service called attendant care, in which the government pays for an attendant to help people who need assistance in their own homes. But at that time (and in numerous cases still) the only way for someone in Nancy's situation to receive attendant care was for him or her to move into the institution where the attendants were employed. So that is what Nancy had to do.

Nancy had experienced many years of institutional existence when ideas about practice and public policy slowly began to change. New attendant programs and other alternatives to institutional care were started. In

Nancy's case, a few visionary social workers and others patched together funding and made arrangements for her to move to her own apartment in a small city, with a personal attendant to assist her. All of those involved, including me, congratulated ourselves on the great victory we had achieved in bringing Nancy to live in a community rather than in the isolating institution.

After a little while, however, my friend Sharon Gretz made an unsettling discovery. Although Nancy and others who had moved with her were *physically* living in a community, they were actually still almost as isolated as they had been when they had lived in an institution. Just as in an institution, everybody who was involved in their lives *was paid to be there.* Unlike Sharon and unlike me, they had no real friends. This led Sharon and other pioneer "askers" to ask ordinary people who lived in the city to become involved in Nancy's life. Since Nancy's faith was very important to her, one of Sharon's friends asked people at a local church if Nancy could attend their church. She started attending weekly services and felt welcome there. She wasn't really involved much, but at least she was present, and that was a first step.

After all those years of isolation and adversity, Nancy was finally tentatively reentering the full life of a town. But at that very moment, her doctors discovered that she had cancer. It was not a type that could be successfully treated, and it seemed she would soon die. At least, everyone thought, her life was not going to end in that institution that had claimed so many of her years.

But this, Sharon discovered to her horror, might not be so. As Nancy became sicker and weaker, she required more hours of attendant care to stay in her home. The agency that paid for her attendants strained its budget to the maximum. Soon, however, it became clear that there would not be enough money to pay for all of the help Nancy needed. When her care became too costly, a situation that takes place with countless old people would occur. Lacking enough money to pay for assistance in her home, Nancy would have to return to the nursing home she had left behind. That was the only place where she could have attendants around-the-clock. That is where she might have to go to die.

Although Nancy was surrounded by very caring and dedicated workers, her situation remained worrisome. Sharon was concerned about Nancy's continuing isolation in her crisis. She had become too sick to get to church services easily, so this promising new avenue of relationships hadn't developed. It occurred to Sharon to try to open things up somehow. In her words:

Nancy and I decided to gather people together to tell the story of how she was feeling. When deciding who to invite, the list was mostly "professionals" who had been in her life at some time—*until*—I was looking at the get-well cards on her wall and saw a name unfamiliar to me. Nancy explained it was a woman from church. She had also brought flowers. We decided to invite her. I called her after looking up her name in the 'phone book. I explained what we wanted to do and asked for her ideas of who else to invite. She thought of the [church] women's circle. We made the invitations.

The first meeting was for Nancy to share where she had been, why she was "missing." The twelve church people who came had wondered where she was (yet didn't inquire far enough). She told them about life in the institution, her dreams and fears. The minister had only been there [for] several weeks. He popped in as we were starting. He said he had seen the invitation, and it intrigued him that such a thing was going on in the church.

At first, the church people saw to it that she was more involved. She went to Bible study, movie night, etc. Then things got worse, and she stopped going.

The unfamiliar card on the wall had led Sharon and Nancy into the heart of the church community. But involvement in activities was no longer enough. Things were becoming desperate. Death in the nursing home loomed, never far out of awareness. Sharon went directly to the minister and explained that what Nancy really needed were people who would come and be with her just because they cared.

This time the minister announced a meeting directly from the pulpit. Again, people came. The minister and Sharon explained the situation—that Nancy needed people to be with her, which would allow her to die at home. The minister handed around a schedule for people to sign up to help for some hours each week. Women volunteered to cook and to clean. Then the list came to a retired fellow named Harry, who had been listening to all of this. "What about you, Harry?" asked the minister.

"I don't know," replied Harry after a bit. "Wouldn't you rather have money? I mean, what do we know about this kind of thing? We don't have any training!"

"The important thing is for Nancy to not approach death alone," explained the minister. "It is important to be with her. To help cook or to clean or help out somehow. You don't need training for that."

"But I don't know anything about cooking or doing laundry," Harry replied.

"Look," the minister finally said, "what Nancy needs even more than cooking and cleaning is somebody to talk with her. Harry, you're the best talker we've got."

So Harry went too.

Once friends from the church started to go to be with Nancy, things changed for her. People brought food and bustled in and out doing things. Someone coordinated a schedule so someone was always with her. Church members were in and out during the day, and staff were there at night or when nobody else could be. And Nancy, although sinking physically, curiously brightened. She started to write poetry.

Finally, lying in bed one day, she confided something to her friends. She told them of a hope she had never uttered aloud. "All my life," she said, "I've wanted a room that was painted a color that *I* picked out. Everyplace I've lived the walls have always been painted with a color that someone else chose. I've always loved canary yellow. Would you paint my room for me?"

So the men got paint samples for her and dragged in their ladders and rollers and brushes, and in quick order the room was done. Nancy lay in her bed in her room, growing steadily weaker, and stared contentedly at her yellow walls, walls surrounding friends both on the staff and from the church. The situation became harder. Some people from the church dropped out because they were afraid she would die when they were there alone. The woman coordinating the schedule found new people to fill in. Some started coming in twos so they would not be alone if something happened. And then Nancy died when Dan, one of the staff members who was closest to her, was there with her, with people from the church expected later in the day.

Nancy's funeral, to which only a few years previously only a few human service workers would have come, had over 40 mourners. There was a dinner in the church basement with an incredible amount of food. Somebody made collages of pictures of Nancy to display, and people stood around them and remembered stories about her together. People wondered what to do about her dearly loved cat, which she would want to be taken care of. So Dan took the cat home to live with him.

It was sad, of course. An early death is sad. But Nancy, who had spent most of her life in isolated care institutions, had done something that is out of the reach of even the very wealthy. She had not died in the hospital or the nursing home, surrounded by paid, if possibly compassionate, strangers working in shifts. She had died in her home. And most remarkably, in this modern age, she had faced death among her friends.

As with the driver of the bus, the action of Nancy's friends was a striking anomaly in the way we ordinarily conceive of what to do in the face of human need. It seems our unexamined assumption, that erecting service systems is the only way to address the needs of people with disabilities in our society, was not necessarily true. Another way existed, that of rediscovering informal ways in which individuals support each other in a community. Despite our inattention to and even dismissal of it, this informal "people's world" could respond in its own way to people in distress.

It became increasingly clear to me while I was directing the council that the distinction between these two different approaches or worlds had nothing specifically to do with people with disabilities or with the field of my daily professional work. Although it is useful to use examples about people like Nancy with disabilities and their communities, it is important for me to be clear that the difference between these two worlds may constitute a much larger question. In fact, one can conceptualize a sharply contrasting relationship between these two worlds, the formal and the informal, in almost all modern settings.

Sam Rogers and the Shin Hollow Library

The little village near which I live part of the time is pretty much just a crossroads on the main highway. Like a lot of small rural towns, it has seen better days. But a few places are still open. There is a bar and a little grocery store, a post office, a hardware store, and the volunteer fire department. In this it is identical to most other villages of its size. But Shin Hollow has one thing many of its neighbors do not: It has a tiny town library. The library is in an old cottage on a side street and is open three afternoons a week. It exists because of one person: Sam Rogers, the town librarian.

Sam is a very interesting character. Primarily she is a goat farmer who wears bib overalls and big muck boots. She has a very gruff voice and long gray hair and smokes a corncob pipe most of the time. Sam is very possibly the best-educated person in town, and she thinks it is important for the town to have a library so the kids can have a place to go after school. Along with running the library and taking care of her goats she also has a greenhouse and is involved in the historical society. She is a center of the community, and she makes her library a center of the community too.

Sam is also an amateur herpetologist, so she is interested in snakes. After school the kids run around in the streams and fields and swamps to find snakes, and then they bring them to Sam at the library. She looks and says, "Well, that's a—wait a minute, let's get out a book," and she looks it up. The snake is squirming around on the library table, and they compare the picture with the snake and find out what it is. That's what a library is for; it's for looking up things you want to know. In Shin Hollow, that's the kind of thing we want to know. It's not the New York Public Library, but it suits us just fine.

What does our library have to do with the two worlds I was talking about? It is this: A few years ago, the state department in charge of libraries announced that it was going to make a new regulation proposing that all libraries in the state would henceforth have to have a librarian with a certified master's degree in library science. If they didn't, the state would cut off their money.

This caused all of us a great deal of consternation. Sam was not a certified librarian, and there was no way she was going to become one. If the state bureaucrats passed this regulation, they were not going to send us money to hire a person with the qualifications they required. And even if they did, what would we do with a certified master's degree librarian in our town? What would such an educated person know about Shin Hollow? What would he or she know about snakes?

If this regulation went through, our library was going to have to close. What was the government trying to do to us?

One thing I was sure of was that the state officials involved and the library association, which I presumed had suggested such a regulation to them, were not trying to hurt our library. I worked in a state government, and I know many people in a lot of state departments. I thought it was more likely that the people in government were genuinely trying to improve our library, but I could not figure out how they were going to do so with this regulation. What picture could they possibly have in their minds of our library that would lead them to believe that this requirement would make our library better?

Finally, I thought I discovered what picture they had of our library. To them, I decided, it must look like Figure 1.1.

This diagram is something I remember from studying physics and engineering and similar subjects. It is a flowchart. Some kind of an input comes in on the left, some process happens to it in the middle, and the resulting output emerges on the right. On the top, some kind of mediating influence affects the way the processing takes place. This type of diagram is very useful for many things. It represents, as contemporary social critic John McKnight pointed out about a similar situation, about the only way you can build automobiles.[2] With automobiles, the steel (and plastic) comes in on the left, and cars roll out on the right. If you want a better car, you increase the specifications of the process on top. For instance, the fed-

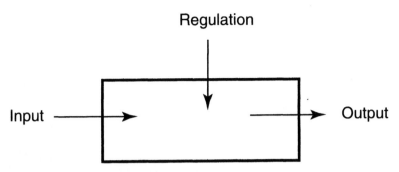

FIGURE 1.1   The Government View of the Shin Hollow Library.
Courtesy of Marcus Schwartz.

eral government decided it wanted safer cars and passed a regulation or law requiring that all cars have air bags. Soon, improved cars with air bags started rolling out of the right side.

Proposing the library regulation I described makes sense only if you see libraries as an input-output process. You decide that the inputs are funding and library materials, and the outputs are information services. This is something you can count. If you want to improve the quality of information services, you increase the specifications of the regulation. Thus, a more technically qualified librarian could only increase the quality—and perhaps the quantity—of the product. Circulation numbers and reference calls become as real a measure of accomplishment as the number of cars produced.

In reality, this is a completely inaccurate diagram of the Shin Hollow library. If you wanted to fit what really takes place in that library into a diagram like the one in Figure 1.1, it would have to look something like Figure 1.2.

As you can imagine, this is a highly simplified diagram of all the things that actually go on in the Shin Hollow library. If you really wanted to track all of the complex interrelationships that take place within the matrix of that setting and around Sam Rogers's involvement with it, you would end up with a diagram that was so full of wiggly arrows that you could no longer see the box. In fact, if you pay attention to the true complexity of the library, a completely different drawing could represent it. That diagram is Figure 1.3.

The figure is meant to be a simple illustration of a beehive. Specifically, it is the part of a hive the beekeeper begins with when he or she wishes to establish a colony. Everyone has probably seen the white boxes of beehives at the edge of clover fields. When the beekeeper places them there, he or she inserts some rectangular wax sheets down into the empty hive. The

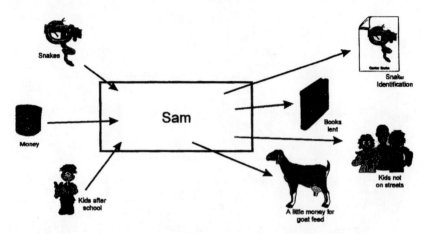

FIGURE 1.2   A More Accurate View of the Shin Hollow Library.
Courtesy of Marcus Schwartz.

sheet has the faint impress of the kind of comb bees actually make. It, together with the presence of the queen, "suggests" to the bees that this
would be a good place to establish a colony, rather than high up in a dead
oak tree where nobody can get to it. For the bees, the wax sheet, which is
called a foundation sheet, is the base upon which their community takes
form.[3]

As G. Scott Williamson and Innes Pearse (whose work I talk about in
Chapter 7) once pointed out, you can think about places in which people
gather in the same way. Sometimes, like beekeepers, you can structure a
place that is so inviting to people (who are as social as bees) that they may
establish a kind of community there. A good example is a corner tavern
"where everybody knows your name," like the one on the popular television show *Cheers,* which is about a community of friends in a bar. A well-
designed and inviting tavern with, most important, a popular bartender
tends to form a community, which in that business is called a bar trade. It
is possible, of course, that someone could try to apply the flowchart diagram to a bar. You could call the inputs thirsty people and full bottles of
beer, and the outputs could be intoxicated people and empty bottles. The
regulation would be the county law that said that people had to stop emp-
tying bottles and start going home by 2:00 A.M. But everybody knows a
bar is not a bottle-emptying station.

With the library, it has been possible to become a bit more confused
than with a bar. It *is* possible to view a library as a flowchart, a kind of
business in which the patrons are customers and the books are raw mate-

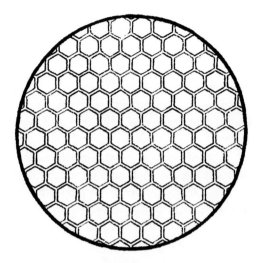

FIGURE 1.3   Beehive Foundation Sheet. Courtesy of Marcus Schwartz.

rials. But it is, I believe, as inaccurate to reduce a library to this description as it is to reduce a bar. Likewise, the events that took place around the life and death of Nancy Lee could not be captured in this way.

The point I wish to make is that this incident, in which my library was viewed as a kind of system illustrated by a flowchart, can serve to show us a process that has taken place regarding all sorts of human enterprises and types of places where people congregate and that is continuing to take place around us all of the time. It is a way to question one of our basic certainties. We are certain, in this modern age, that many of the social institutions around us can be understood as flowcharts of one kind or another. This is particularly true of any kind of social enterprise whose purpose is to take care of people. We have come to call these kinds of efforts, in their aggregate, "human services."[4]

Underground in the Asylum

My first job in human services was in a state mental hospital. I went there looking for a summer job mowing lawns, for I had noticed wide expanses of lawn between all of the old buildings. But they were so pleased to see an applicant with a college degree that they immediately offered me a job as a rehabilitation counselor. So I ended up trying to figure out how to help people with severe mental disorders rather than mowing lawns.

I vividly remember walking through the massive oak doors of the old asylum building for the first time. The asylum, which was built in 1869, looked like Figure 1.4.

In this building, and in the many others erected during the one hundred years following its establishment, a vast program for people with mental illness was managed. For a young person who had never seen the inside of such an institution, the experience was disorienting. There was, on the one hand, the individual and collective effect of so many people who were very disturbed. But even more striking was the impression of suddenly being a part of the massive and weighty machinery by which this large institution was operated in all of its exquisite detail—regulation of the daily caloric intake of patients, medication administration, the calculation of salaries and leave times, and even the eventual burials in unmarked but numbered plots in the institution's cemetery.

I do not need to tell you that this was not a good place for a person with a mental disorder to be. I could write a book about the terrible things I saw happen to people there—the anguish, the massive drugging, the imprison-

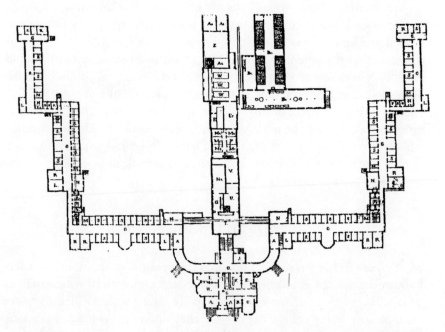

FIGURE 1.4   The Willard Asylum, 1869. Courtesy of the Willard Asylum, Willard, NY, c. 1869.

ments, the sad deaths. Yet the employees were not evil people. In fact, I met a number of compassionate and gifted people there. (Such people, of course, exist in all settings, even those far worse than that state hospital.)

All of the bad things that happened to patients at the state hospital in the hands of reasonably nice people took place as an expression of well-established rules and procedures for the treatment of mental illness and the administration of institutions for these patients' care. As I realized sometime later, the state hospital was a setting predicated on the assumption that the treatment of mental illness could fairly be described and carried out following the idea of an input-output chart. People admitted with mental illness were inputs, and people who were discharged were outputs. Thus rules, as in the mediating arrow on the diagram I used in Figure 1.1, were the logical way by which the process taking place in the institution was controlled. It operated like a factory; like all factories, it was a large machine.

There are two simple ways to see whether an enterprise planned to care for people is designed as a machine. You can take two "X rays" of the setting that will reveal, as X rays do, its inner structure. The first X ray is a cross section of the building, as it appears in Figure 1.4. This is a picture, as John McKnight might put it, of a "machine for caring." Like all nineteenth-century asylum structures, it is an especially clear picture of an environmental machine. Erected following the generally accepted design specifications of 1869, the building held wards in which inmates with different types of insanity could be domiciled according to diagnosis. In the center shaft of the device all of the central support services were housed: the pharmacy, bakery, chapel, and kitchens. This is one way of seeing how people were organized.

A second and even clearer way to see how people were organized would be to take an X ray that ignored buildings and focused solely on lines of authority: who was able to direct whom. In the 1869 asylum, the resulting image would have looked something like Figure 1.5.

This figure, as McKnight first pointed out to me, is very familiar. It is the way all bureaucracies are structured. In such an organization, the box does the work. In the personnel office at the asylum, my box said "rehabilitation counselor," and I was the employee hired to fill that station, just as at the auto plant. At this institution and in the state mental hygiene system, such boxes, or jobs, were referred to by the term *items*. If as a supervisor I wanted to give two people raises, I said to the personnel office that I "wanted to upgrade two items." People were not mentioned; only the boxes into which they fit in the organization chart were discussed.

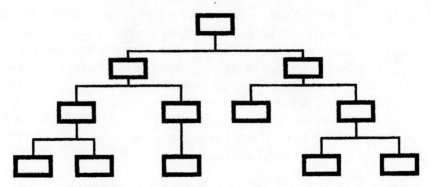

FIGURE 1.5   Organization Chart. Courtesy of the author.

One thing that is particularly striking about institutions of this time period is that if you hold the two X rays—that of the building and that of the people—side by side, they rather resemble each other.

The results of the professional caring system these diagrams illustrate were, from the point of view of the person with mental illness subject to that system, pretty unpleasant.[5] It was not designed to be like this, of course. The system had been designed to be a model of humanitarian care, and for a few short years after its founding, it was so. By the time I encountered it, however, this system had been administering a terrible experience to its inmates for many decades. I came during a successful period of reform, and the time in which people had been kept naked and been hosed down was a few years past. We now had a more modern complex of programs and therapies. I, as a new staff person, was trying to learn how to become a contributing member of this remodeled professional service system. Yet I couldn't help noticing that even this new system didn't seem to be doing that much good for the people in its charge. What was wrong?

Much has been written about the problems of institutions and their reform. Could the hospital have been organized and structured in a better way so a higher quality of service would be delivered to the patients? At the time I was there, I thought that faulty structure was the problem and even proposed ways of changing the structure so things would be better.

Now that I have witnessed and carried out many reorganizations, it is much clearer to me that changes in structure leave the most important determining aspects of these places unchanged. Let me give an example. Back then, when I once complained that a patient was losing weight because he was not getting enough to eat, I received a stinging memo from the physician in charge of the ward telling me to stick to my own profession, which did not include the science of nutrition, as did hers. She was warning me to stay in my own box in the organization chart and not to stray into hers. No matter how many times you reorganized the boxes in the chart, you would still have an organization made up of boxes in which things like this would—and, I learned, must—occur. Working as part of an organization chart, in other words, describes a certain type of relationship among people—a formal one in which individuals relate to each other in prescribed ways, autonomy is limited, and directions flow from top to bottom.

In Chapter 2 I talk about why the situation of the state hospital is far from unique in being a large organized structure that produces negative results despite aiming for positive ones. But for the moment I want to be clear that I am only talking about certain *aspects* of the situation in the hospital, in which two different ways of responding to people can be seen most clearly.

I encountered a contrasting way of thinking about people in the hospital in a curious way. One of my jobs was to go to the wards and interview new admissions and suggest referral to suitable rehabilitation programs. I was doing this one day when a seemingly disconnected event ended up changing my life. A patient named Owen Zerling fell off the back of a laundry truck and was hurt. Unknown to me, this incident precipitated a small institutional reform. The following day I was placed in charge of the program that supervised patient workers, with orders to stop the usage of patient labor for institutional purposes and change it to a program of therapeutic benefit to them. As a first step, I visited all of the places where patients worked in the hospital. This was like stepping through the looking glass. Leaving the known world of managed wards and professional clinics, I found myself in a completely different world that existed silently beneath the official reality of the psychiatric hospital.

My tour of workplaces took me inside all of the places professional therapists never see. Underneath the world of the wards was a vast network of kitchens, bakeries, and greenhouses, of plumbing shops and photography offices. And there was the basement where the men who cut the grass on the institution director's golf course hung out. Here, with them, were lots of patients I had never seen on the wards. It was a different world, and it functioned by different rules.

Among these bakers, groundspeople, and other "support" workers at the institution, I started to realize, was a variety of people whose presence and interest seemed to naturally help to heal those suffering from mental disturbances. Most of these latter individuals, I came to learn, seemed to be suffering chiefly because of the lack of any role other than being a mental patient. Seeing this, I began to look at my work differently. I started to match up newly admitted patients with some of these "natural therapists" I had gotten to know.

A retired woman, who was seriously depressed, was admitted. I talked with her and found that all of her children were grown and gone; she had nothing else to do with her life. Had she ever worked before her marriage, long ago? It turned out that she had worked briefly as a bookkeeper, but that was so long ago that she thought she would be of no use at it today. "Well," I replied, "nonetheless, maybe you would be willing to help us while you are here. Our dentist is terribly short staffed, and his records are a mess. Could you help him out a few hours a day? We could pay you a little." Over her feeble protests that she could be of no worth to anyone, I extracted an agreement that she would at least meet the dentist.

Then I ran down to the dentist, a friend of mine, and persuaded him of how much he needed to help the woman out by having her in his office. I got her started working there and put her on the payroll. A few weeks later when I visited the woman, I found her flourishing, kidding around with the other secretaries, beaming at the attention of the dentist, happy with his improved records. And somehow, her depression had been relieved sufficiently (no doubt because of the effectiveness of the antidepressants!) that she did not need electroshock therapy after all.

Through countless opportunities like this one, I began to learn the dimensions of the subterranean world that existed beneath the professional and systemic one. By virtue of my job, I held the sole professional "passport" to visit this other world. One by one, I took patients there and introduced them. A young woman with a terribly severe psychosis would end up with the lady who cleaned the nursing school, a woman of infinite patience and understanding who soon started taking the younger woman home for lunch and even for Christmas. A young man would end up with the photographer, because the latter was especially good with adolescents. Another fellow would leave the wards for the cellar of the maintenance shed, where the greenspeople stashed their secret barrel of hard cider.

I knew this other, hidden world, far beneath the surface of institutional life, was a different one. I knew people acted differently here than elsewhere in the hospital. I knew I liked it and that the patients I took there liked it, too. Thinking back on my vivid memories of those times, I would phrase a description of the difference of this world from the other world in the terms I am using today. I would say that this world, too, like my library, could not be described as a flowchart or a formal system. This world, with all of its messy realities, was an informal one where the actions of people could not be readily predicted. If the institution was made of neat stone blocks, this world was the blades of grass that were sprouting up between the stones.

In this chapter I have spoken of four very different situations to try to show how, in each setting, the difference between the two worlds I mentioned at the start can be seen. On the one hand, there is a way of responding to what we call human need by erecting a formal system of service. On the other, there is a way of responding to people in personal, nonsystemic ways, ways that are shaped and patterned by the informal ways of relating to each other that arise from a people's historical learning.

In the mental hospital, with its two worlds, one can see today a reflection of the entire society. As in the institution, our ideas of how we respond to the situation of other people are shaped mostly by formal systematic procedures that constitute one of our most basic modern certainties. Standing upon this certainty, we can miss the existence of an alternative way of living that is located beneath it. In the mental hospital, I referred to this as a subterranean world. But it would be more accurate, I think, to refer to it as a subinstitutional world.

The shape of our lives is defined by our insertion into institutions and systems whose interlocking power generates the "virtual reality" we experience. It is this reality that moves us to pick up the phone and dial 911 when we see the woman on the bridge rather than rush out to save her. It is this reality that causes parents and pediatricians to "know" one must administer strong antibiotics for young children's routine ear infections, when many simpler—and safer!—home treatments often work as well. Such "knowledge" is so thoroughly a part of our worldview that it simply would not occur to most people to question it. Yet underneath this reality is another, subinstitutional reality in which very different responses are simply acted out. This is the reality in which everyone, until very recently, lived.

In Chapter 2, I examine the formal idea and its consequences. What are some of the effects of our current beliefs about caring? What are the results of thinking that, again in McKnight's words, a formal system can render care?[6]

t w o

THE LITTLE BOY WHO WAS
AFRAID OF WHITE

So persuasive is the power of the institutions we have created that they shape not only our preferences, but actually our sense of possibilities.

—Ivan Illich

For man has closed himself up till he sees all things through the chinks of his cabin.

—William Blake

Some months ago, while traveling, I received an urgent telephone call from an old friend who had managed to locate me. He was calling about his brother Tom, who was in serious trouble. My friend hadn't known where his brother was for a long time. Tom had traveled constantly for all of his adult life. Recently, my friend had received a call from a police station, where Tom was behaving in a seriously disturbed way. Over the succeeding weeks, this situation was repeated in city after city, in crisis after crisis. My friend and I worked together, trying to understand what might be happening and to figure out how to get Tom some help he might accept.

Over the course of our conversations, I gradually learned the story of a man without a home. With only a simple suitcase that invariably held the same items, without friends or the many other relationships most people take for granted, Tom had traveled for years from place to place—living in residential hotels, getting to know no one, and ready to move on at the slightest indication that something appeared threatening. That sense of threat seemed now to be expanding to the point where it dominated Tom's perception of the world, and his consequent behavior was bringing him to the police, jails, and mental hospitals.

The story I learned was complex and fascinating. But one aspect of it particularly moved me. Tom had been born fifty years ago very prematurely. Ordinarily, back then babies that premature didn't live. But Tom's parents were fortunate to live near a major medical center in which techniques for saving premature infants were being pioneered. The center had special incubators to keep such babies alive. Tom was the most premature baby the hospital, at that point, had ever saved. In the process of this rescue, however, he had spent most of his first year in the white world of the hospital incubator. His sheets were white, the room was white, the doctors' and nurses' uniforms were white. This was back in the time when doctors and nurses had just learned how to keep premature infants alive but hadn't yet realized how crucial it was for babies to be touched and held and loved. So nobody had touched Tom or held him or loved him during that entire first year. He lay on his back in the bright lights of the intensive care nursery and breathed the oxygenated air and gazed out upon his white world. Finally, when he was strong enough, he was able to go home. When he arrived at home, his parents discovered a curious thing: Tom was deathly afraid of the color white.

This, Tom's brother told me, was one of his earliest memories of his brother: that everything around him had to be colored, or he would scream and scream. Even his milk had to have a few drops of food coloring put into it, or he would not drink it.

This story is important, of course, for understanding Tom, particularly from the viewpoint of a therapist who might attempt to penetrate the mystery of his life: why he was compelled by fear to construct such a narrow existence, why he had apparently never developed the capacity to form the close relationships with people that constitute the greatest gifts in this challenging and often lonely life, and how he might be helped through the opportunity of this current crisis to a fuller and more rewarding existence. Yet Tom's story can have a more general meaning as well. It is an example of the curious and tragic fact now coming to people's awareness about places that provide care: They can produce negative as well as positive results. In Tom's case, the positive result was unambiguous: He is alive only because of the medical technology that saved him. But the unexpected negative effects of living in this exclusively technological and institutional world—this white world—helped to create a serious impairment to his growth and development. Certain other infants back then were saved by the oxygen in the incubators, but too much oxygen caused them to go blind, a condition called retrolental fibroplasia. What happened to them and what happened to Tom was essentially the same kind of thing, only in Tom's case the result was less immediately obvious.

With the use of oxygen, one could make the case that negative effects could not have been foreseen. But in the case of Tom, the behavior of the medical personnel raises a disturbing question. How did presumably interested doctors and nurses get the idea that you didn't have to touch, hold, and love little babies, no matter what the nature of their physical problems? Surely many of these professionals had children of their own. How could they have come to think that the affection all infants have received from their mothers from time immemorial could simply be dispensed with? Somehow, one must conclude, their fervent desire to help babies through the use of medical technology drowned out their commonsense knowledge that leaving infants lying alone would surely have bad effects. Without some understanding about how this unusual conduct originated, the behavior of such people in the name of care is simply inexplicable. This history is taken up in Chapter 5.[1]

Iatrogenesis and Counterproductivity

The existence of negative effects following medical care is not new. Further, the daily press is full of upsetting discoveries about medical procedures or drugs that have turned out to cause serious injuries as well as confer benefits: the drug DES, breast implants, and hospital-caused infections, to name just a few. As these problems increased, along with dramatic advances in the power of medical intervention, widespread awareness brought an old term into more common use: *iatrogenic,* or "doctor-caused," illness. Over the years, evidence of the negative effects of medical care increased to the point that by 1976, Ivan Illich, in his book *Medical Nemesis: The Expropriation of Health,* proclaimed the existence of what he called an "iatrogenic pandemic."[2] He felt, in other words, that the negative effects of medical care had become so pervasive and profound that if they were more fully recognized, a major new "threat to health" would be declared.

I mention iatrogenic medicine because it is one of the earliest instances of recognition of a wider phenomenon: the emerging and unsettling awareness that caring professions and institutions can produce effects that are the opposite of those for which they aim. Iatrogenesis helped to open up the much larger issue of the counterproductive effects of what I will call, in the broadest sense of the term, the *institutions of modern society*.

The state hospital about which I spoke in Chapter 1 is one concrete example of such an institution in its most extreme counterproductive form. This is the reason, although I didn't realize it at the time, the frequent reorganizations of structure it underwent never produced any appreciable improvement. The reorganizations I dreamed up wouldn't have improved the situation much, either. The problem was located in the very nature of the enterprise itself.[3] Although asylums had started with strong humanitarian intentions and had in fact bestowed considerable benefits upon inmates when they were new, by the time they became large and bureaucratically organized, such benefits had essentially faded. Eventually, the people who were admitted were worse off in these places than they had been before. Strangely, the hospital somehow became a machine for *producing* mental illness.[4] As treatment failures accumulated, the numbers of deadened, institutionalized people became larger, as did the institution itself and the mental health system of which it was a part. By the time I entered the field in 1970, it was recognized that the primary problem of the thousands of people incarcerated in mental institutions was not mental disorder but institutionalization—a condition created by the treatment facility itself.

Various social observers started to notice that the phenomenon in which an institution produced the opposite of its stated intentions could be seen in a wide variety of social settings. Institutions, once they passed a certain threshold of size and intensity, seemed to become inverted in their results. Schools made people stupid. Medicine made them sick. Prisons created criminals.[5] Illich gave this phenomenon the term *paradoxical counterproductivity*.

As modern institutions tend to produce the opposite of their stated purpose, they also tend to eliminate possibilities for other kinds of action. Illich names the situation in which one type of institutional product displaces all other possibilities a *radical monopoly*.[6] When I take the train to New Haven to visit a friend, for instance, it is not possible for me to walk from the train station to my hotel, although the distance is not great. Walking is no longer feasible because the space in between the two spots has been filled with superhighway ramps, erected to enable cars to travel easily. Even imagining the possibility of walking has become impossible. In this case, you can say a radical monopoly exists because the presence of automobiles and their support systems has actually eliminated the possibility of using one's feet. Natural competence, in Illich's words, has been ruled out.[7]

The state mental hospital where I worked was established to help people with mental disorders.[8] In the very beginning, as I mentioned, it did so. But when a few decades had gone by and it had become the largest mental institution in the Western world, its path toward producing the opposite results for its inmates was beginning to be well-worn. Paradoxical counterproductivity had set in.

In addition, however, the ever-enlarging presence of the state hospital exerted a gravitational influence on the surrounding community through its physical size and economic power, so that the range of problems for which it was seen as the solution was expanded. Thus, the custom was established of sending anyone to the asylum who showed signs of what might possibly appear to be mental illness. Old people were routinely dropped off by their families when they began to need someone to be with them and to help them with small tasks.[9] When those of us involved in the deinstitutionalization movement began to try to move people out of the now admittedly scandalous institutions, we found communities in which native capacities to support such people had considerably withered. The radical monopoly of institutional care had eliminated fragile informal capacities to include people that had existed prior to these artificial creations. It was now as difficult to consider the possibility of helping a person with a disability to live in an ordinary neighborhood as it was to consider walking from the New Haven train station to the Holiday Inn.

In Chapter 1 I delineated two different ways of responding to the situation of people who appear to be in need. The dominant way, I pointed out, is the formal approach typified by the input-output chart, or the organizational chart. After years of development, social institutions driven by this approach have become not only virtually the sole social response to vulnerable people but have also become so pervasive that they determine even our sense of the possibilities of what can be done. This is why one, without thinking, dials 911 in response to a suicide attempt or mandates certification for a librarian in response to a desire to improve libraries. Yet all of these systems—as they have reached a threshold combination of size, professionalism, and density of rules—working over time, have become afflicted with paradoxical counterproductivity, somehow turning means into ends and beginning to deliver the opposite of their stated mandates. We live in a world characterized by these all-pervasive, nonworking systems. The effect of such counterproductivity is felt most keenly by those among us who are dependent upon social services of various kinds for their continued existence.[10]

Entering Virtual Reality

We have a new airport in Harrisburg. In the old one—a large Quonset hut left over from World War II—you had to walk across the tarmac and up the stairway to your plane. If it was raining, somebody handed you a big umbrella when you walked out the door, and another airline employee took it as you entered the plane. But now we have a new, gleaming airport with up-to-date ramps that connect with the planes. I can walk into the airport, down the ramp, and into the plane, change planes in Pittsburgh or Chicago, and emerge in San Francisco or Frankfurt or London without leaving an air-conditioned environment for a single moment. With the completion of our Harrisburg ramps, my experience of machine-processed air is now continuous, seamless.

I travel a considerable amount, and I notice that it is not only the experience of air travel that has become seamless and continuous; it is the entire world through which I make my way. All of it is exact and familiar. There are the same aircraft, the same chain restaurants, the same newspaper stands. The stands, with minor regional variations, have the same national newspapers, the same magazines, the same candy. At a large airport, if you don't find what you want to drink at one of the bars, you won't find it at any other, because they are all managed by the same corporation and have the same stock. When I am deceived with unadvertised add-on charges at a rental car counter in Florida, I am experiencing the same deception I would have encountered if I had taken the plane to Seattle instead and rented from the same company. The efficient rental agent is not cheating me with the personal canniness of the carpet salesperson at the bazaar; the agent's is an entirely impersonal act that has been computer simulated and fiscally overseen and for which the person before me has been carefully educated through a standardized training program. As long as I travel in the continuous tube of airport–plane–onboard movie–rental car–hotel–chain restaurant–airport, I experience only carefully overseen manifestations of a single managed reality. In this reality, it is very unusual to encounter a surprise. The possibility of surprises has been assiduously kept to a minimum.

If you were to take the kind of X ray of this travel world that I applied to the state mental hospital in Chapter 1, the image that emerged would look almost exactly the same. The travel world would appear as an almost incredibly detailed complexity of input-output charts and flowcharts. If you asked every single person you encountered on a trip if they worked for themselves or were employees of a corporation, you would almost certainly find that you were talking to an employee of a corporation who carried out a designed role in an organization chart. The tremendous sophistication of all of the interlocking institutional systems involved makes possible that which I experience as a traveler: the completely predictable, regular, artificial reality that is generated within the continuous travel tube by the institutions that compose it. Thousands of skilled systems managers work constantly to expand and refine this desired artificial reality and to quickly fill any gaps that might remain, such as one in which my feet might touch the earth or my head could be soaked by rain.[11]

In the modern world of computer simulations, there is a parallel to the artificial travel world: the expanding field of virtual reality. A virtual reality can be created in a basic form, for instance, by a flight-training simulator. A pilot in training goes into a large metal box in a windowless room and sits down in a real cockpit for a certain kind of plane. A computer then simulates an entire flight, including what is seen out of the windshield, the readings on all of the instruments, the messages on the radio, even the tilt and rocking of the plane in bad weather. Near disasters, such as engine failures, can be simulated so convincingly in such devices that seasoned pilots have been seen emerging from such trials drenched with sweat. They have "known," of course, that they are safely on the concrete floor of the training room, but all of their senses have been so carefully exploited that a real airplane flight is the unshakable reality they experience.

In the laboratories of virtual reality studies, computers can be harnessed to create even broader and more convincing realities. Ways will be found for machines to interface more directly with the senses or even with nerve endings. The future will produce an astonishing variety of simulations that can be created—virtually—out of a machine.

The continuous travel tube, although bulky, is one variety of virtual reality. It, too, is created by systems projecting onto the senses, although here the systems are the carefully managed interrelationships of people. This travel world, as a virtual reality, is as certain in one's experience as the ground upon which one walks. A human being raised entirely within this world would have no way of knowing that earth turns to mud when it rains or that people are not always evaluated annually on their job performance or that every person is not always viewed and treated as a potentially dangerous criminal or terrorist.

Our modern world, based largely upon such institutionally created certainties, is such a virtual reality. From this standpoint, the airport world is merely a concrete example of such a reality. In this larger virtual reality, certain things are accepted as self-evident. We know, for example, that when you need to learn things you enroll in school, follow a curriculum, and receive something called credits. We know that when your baby doesn't seem to be eating well you ask a pediatrician, not your grandmother, what to do. We are told that if you are depressed it is important to recognize that you have a medical illness and that you should see a doctor for antidepressants. We know that when you are old and sick you go to a nursing home. We know that if you see a woman about to attempt suicide on a bridge you should dial 911. We know countless things, in this virtual reality, about how you should deal with all of the many problems of living. The reason we know these things so clearly is that the knowledge has been provided in a seamless and convincing way by the institutions that take charge of—even colonize—each realm of human experience. To me, one passes into the world of virtual reality once the density of flowcharts and organization charts reaches a certain threshold. Past this point, nothing but virtual reality can exist.

I have spoken about the world of airports and travel only to illustrate the densely managed virtual reality in which we live. This reality extends as well to the world of my professional interests, that of human services and social service endeavors. This is the world you may enter if you attempt to jump from a bridge or are born with a disability. Unlike the travel world, however, this world is not sparklingly efficient. In this world the person behind the counter may not be well trained. In this world the toilets may not be clean.

The person walking into the disability system, I have slowly realized, now encounters the same density of artificially managed reality as the airline traveler. Instead of programmed rental agents and cabin attendants, however, one may encounter overworked caseworkers. Instead of a destination sticker, one is given a diagnosis. One might not actually get anywhere, because the virtual reality of human services is, by and large, the low-rent end of the reality of which airports are the pinnacle. And it is here that the phenomenon of paradoxical counterproductivity is a crushingly unavoidable presence. In the world of human services, dysfunctional practices can routinely become the standard—mixing counterproductivity and monopoly in an ever-enlarging sphere, displacing all ordinary ways of living, acting, feeling, knowing, grieving, living with others, or caring for others. The result, frequently, is a kind of learned helplessness. People become unable to even *imagine* that other alternatives are possible.[12]

Deinstitutionalization

I learned this fact with particular force in the years after I left my work at the state hospital. It had become clear to me there that reform of the structure was impossible. What was essential was to get people *out*, out to the rich and unpredictable experiences of everyday community life. It was just at the time in which the community mental retardation movement was starting to reshape public policy. I had the opportunity to start some community residences in the heart of a nearby city. We leased and renovated some houses on residential streets and welcomed former patients into ordinary life. It was a grand and exciting enterprise, and on the whole it worked out exceedingly well. But after some years of being involved in this new, "alternative" movement, I noticed something that seemed rather strange.

When some of us first began to set up these kinds of arrangements, there was no "field" of community services. There were no training programs, no professional associations or journals, no approved management methods. My office was located in the den of the first group home; our bookkeeper worked on the kitchen table. Like all new enterprises, it was rather chaotic. There were no rules, and we had to feel our way with every step. But everybody involved—residents, staff, board members, myself—flourished wildly. We worked hard to get to where things were organized. I developed lots of procedures and systems. It was not just this way for me: Everybody who was doing the same thing at the time was living under the same crazy conditions and working hard to achieve structure and organization.

Now, fifteen years later, I see that my colleagues and I were incredibly successful. The community residential enterprise in mental retardation is a well-developed, complex system with university degree programs, its own computer management software, client records systems, behavorial consultants, and state and federal regulations. These were originally supposed to be real homes in which everybody, staff and residents, lived together. This was the desire of parents, who envisioned their adult children living as closely as possible to the way they did rather than in the isolation and regimentation of institutional life. Yet today I find that the idea of staff living with residents, following the ideal of creating a real home, has almost completely vanished. Homes are staffed in shifts, just like the institution. And the requirements of regulations seem to be on everyone's lips.

This situation was brought home to me recently when a staff member of a group home called me with a problem. She had made a friend at the group home in which she worked and wanted to invite her home on Sundays and accompany her to church. This seemed like a great thing to do, but she had been told by the agency administrators that it was prohibited. Since the friend was an agency client, if the off-duty staff member were to spend time with the client she would have to be paid, or she would be violating federal labor policy. She didn't work on weekends and the agency didn't have the money to pay her overtime, so she simply was not permitted to spend time with the client. I checked into the situation and found, to my amazement, that according to the law the agency was correct. What had happened to the wonderfully messy world of group homes in which pursuing a friendship was not prohibited?

This brings to mind the image of a rock garden. Why do gardeners pile up rock terraces? The answer is, to make beds for flowers to bloom. In community agencies, structure was analogous to the rocks in a rock garden. Relationships were the flowers. The growth and healing in group homes of people with mental retardation and other disabilities took place not because of agency structure or structured programs but through living relationships with staff, friends, and neighbors. The purpose of agency structure was to provide a setting in which this healing could optimally take place, just as the proper arrangement of rock terraces helps flowers to grow beautifully. What was happening all around me, I could now see, was that the rocks had received all of the emphasis. The rock-to-flower ratio had surreptitiously become heavily weighted on the side of rocks.

If you saw a gardener who had somehow formed the idea that rock gardens were not about flowers but about rocks and had piled up rocks until the soil and flowers were squeezed out, it would be immediately apparent that something was seriously wrong. In the realm of human services, where rocks and flowers are not as obvious to see, the rocks were taking over the garden. The flowering of friendship was starting to be against the rules. One could see here how the world of the flowchart was expanding—even in the newest liberating enterprises—and the world of friendship and community was consequently diminishing. By what processes is the informal world of relationships being continually displaced?

three

HOW INFORMAL LIFE
IS DROWNED

In Chapter 1 I proposed the beehive as an image to depict the world of informal relationships as opposed to the world governed by inputs and outputs, the world of 911. I suggested that understanding the difference between these two ways of viewing the world was necessary for understanding our current habits of response to the situation of people we perceive as having needs. It is possible to see that the world composed of systems has in many ways become almost completely dominant and that its monopoly of possibilities increases despite its escalating counterproductivity. Further, one can also observe that as the formal world of the input-output chart becomes larger, the informal world represented by the image of the beehive diminishes.

When Illich talks about what I call the beehive, he uses a specific term: *vernacular*. This word is familiar in everyday language because of the term *vernacular speech*, which describes the everyday language of a place. *Vernacular*, Illich wrote, "comes from an Indo-Germanic root that implies 'rootedness' and 'abode.' *Vernaculum* as a Latin word was used for whatever was homebred, homespun, homegrown, homemade, as opposed to what was obtained in formal exchange."[1] The story I told about Nancy dying in the arms of her friends was something that took place almost completely in the vernacular world. In the airport, nothing remains of the world of the vernacular; it has all been displaced by systems.[2]

The squeezing out of space for soil and flowers by expanding piles of rocks is a metaphor for the displacement of the vernacular that can be seen in all arenas of modern life. Each year more and more of the world passes out of the sphere of the vernacular and into the sphere of systems. Mom-and-pop stores fall to chain convenience stores, the neighborhood doctor and midwife become employees of health maintenance organizations, and small-scale, personal efforts to help people become human service corporations. In all of these, the same process of a war against the simple subsistence focus of the vernacular can be observed.

Market Economics

The dynamics of how this uncontrolled expansion of the world of systems devours the vernacular are fairly complex to trace, and Illich has spent considerable effort attempting to discern how this accepted aspect of the modern world came into being. The leading factor, he has come to believe, is the way market-driven economics became unbridled as a force shaping society. A starting point for his thinking was a book by Karl Polanyi called *The Great Transformation: The Political and Economic Origins of Our Time.*[3]

Today, we are used to the dominance of economics and economic thinking. We have grown up with things like cost-benefit ratios that boil all aspects of existence down to economics. Economics has become our common and familiar language. But this is actually an exceedingly strange way of looking at the world and is one with serious repercussions. Chief among these is the way such a view fuels the displacement of vernacular existence. As David Cayley summarized: "As the economy expands, Illich says, it sucks the marrow from culture and community. People cease to do for themselves what others now do for them, for a price. Natural competence decays, institutions expand."[4]

The idea that free-market economics should be the standard for assessing all problems resulted in a new creed that, in Polanyi's words, "was utterly materialistic and believed that all human problems could be resolved given an unlimited amount of material commodities."[5] It is as if a particular infection, long held in balance by natural forces, were to spread to infect the whole of human existence. Once the infection became a universal aspect of shared reality, nobody would then perceive it as an infection. When I was a little boy, I thought it was natural that the hillside behind our house was covered with honeysuckle, covering over all but the highest trees. I didn't realize that the honeysuckle had started with a single rooting planted to hide an outhouse, to which the natural ecology of the woods had little resistance.[6]

In recent years, I have become very attentive to the ways in which economic thinking appears in efforts to help people. With many human services, it is clear that a transformation has taken place in intent, paralleling that of the state hospital. Behind the "mask of love," as John McKnight so eloquently put it, we increasingly find a large industrial system that requires people's needs as raw material to fuel corporate growth.[7] Often this is rather unambiguous. Staff social workers who find new clients for nursing homes, for instance, are sometimes termed "buyers."[8] Through this process in which needs are turned into commodities and help into human resources, what I have elsewhere called the "commodification of everyday life" expands. A smaller and smaller space exists for the vernacular, "the domain in which culture still holds the economy at bay."[9]

Plastic Words

A particularly striking method by which the degradation of the vernacular occurs has recently been brought to light by German scholar Uwe Pörksen. It has to do with what we can notice about the use of words. Pörksen noticed that if you listened to conversations in any field and even in any language, you tended to hear the same words used again and again regardless of the topic. Some of these words, for instance, were *sexuality, communication, information, needs, system, problem, function, model,* and *project.* With careful study, Pörksen was able to identify a list of thirty or forty such words and to specify their peculiar characteristics. He called these plastic words.[10]

Plastic words, Pörksen discovered, were words borrowed from science that when used in popular speech connote much but denote little. They connote, for instance, the prestige of science; although they may actually stand for little in factual content, no one notices. A common sentence using plastic words, for instance, might be: "Increased communication about needs is the best strategy for an educational project." One can sit in a conference or read professional journals and find statements like this all the time. Such statements can just as easily, as Pörksen showed, be said in another order and sound equally meaningful: "Educational strategies are the best way to increase communication about needs."

Pörksen's elegant formulation cannot be adequately described here. But it is important to mention his discovery if we want to see clearly how the vernacular is, in his words, "softened up" and "colonized." These are the words through which the vernacular world has been made over into the virtual reality in which we now live. Of these words he says, "They can be compared to the floats of a fishing-net. They are not isolated; they are much rather like nodal points connected by a web of criss-crossing links. The result is a net drawn over and perhaps even holding captive our consciousness of the world."[11]

The world I have attempted to describe in the preceding pages—in which the vernacular is displaced by economic systems, colloquial words are displaced by plastic ones, and "beehives" are displaced by flowcharts—is the world in which those of us concerned with responding to the vulnerabilities and injuries of people now do our work. This is why that work has become so curiously difficult at a time when gains in economic and political power have been achieved by certain groups long ignored, such as individuals with disabilities.

For many years I oversaw the awarding of grants to many small groups of people who wished to start organizations to help people. In many of these organizations, a very similar thing happened. In the metaphor of the rock garden, they often developed an oversupply of rocks surprisingly early in their organizational lives. One began to hear plastic words in the speech of those who were starting the organizations. Soon, I learned, paradoxical counterproductivity inevitably followed. Organizations must exert an enormous effort to counter the tendency, at times the pressure, to succumb to the nearly universal fate of such enterprises.

Almost nobody under age thirty has seen that once ubiquitous tree known as the American elm. They all died, we know, of Dutch elm disease. Most people believe that all elms not artificially maintained with fungicides are long dead. The fact is a little different: All elms not so maintained over a certain *age and size* are dead.

If you walk in the woods, you can still spot an occasional American elm seedling coming up. They live to a certain point and *then* die of the disease. Looking at seedlings in the woods, I am often reminded of fledgling social service settings making their spirited starts before systemic infection takes its toll.

No matter how difficult the times, the impulse of people to help one another goes on at some level, even though it may be so diminished that only vestiges remain. There can be no doubt that these times are difficult. Most of the institutions of modern society are deteriorating rapidly, brought low by counterproductivity and their own monopolistic success. Now that the response to need has been so thoroughly commodified, economic crises increase, for constantly increasing our resources has become the only way to respond. As formal systems expand and become the only source of support, people are increasingly left alone. When they have difficulties, there is no longer an informal or vernacular world to turn to. All they can do—all they can imagine doing—is to call upon a system for care. A local fire chief in Maryland, for instance, appealing for an increase in his budget for ambulance services, reported that one lonely woman had been responsible for 147 emergency calls in the past year. She had been having panic attacks.

In the virtual reality we have created, one may end up calling the ambulance crew to reassure oneself in the middle of one's lonely, fearful nights. People do so because in our managed virtual reality of human service systems they can find themselves utterly alone. They are as alone as the infant Tom was in his white incubator in his white hospital, surrounded by the whiteness of systems but without the touch of his mother and his family. How he must have instinctively longed for them, there in the midst of his life-support systems!

Thanks to those systems, he lived, but somehow he ended up terribly afraid. He ended up afraid of the color white, which can represent the artificial world that is all institutions, even at their best, can create. But sadly, he ended up apparently afraid of the touch of others as well, which is why he always had to move, why he had no friends.

Tom's life is, perhaps, a metaphor for our own plight. Like him, there are some signs that people are becoming deeply afraid of the benefits of caring systems. We have seen the sudden appearance of living wills. A book on suicide to avoid prolonged medical treatment when you are dying becomes an instant best-seller. Articles on the injuries that can befall one in hospitals or schools fill the daily papers. And like Tom, too, we seem to be becoming more fearful and suspicious of each other.

Yet the infant Tom and the adult Tom always, in his heart, must have longed for the company of others. Men and women are vernacular creatures. They naturally live in communities as surely as bees congregate in beehives. When they do not have the experience of community they almost invariably long for it, although sometimes in distorted and almost incomprehensible ways, such as calling an ambulance squad. It is thus perhaps in response to the virtual whiteness of modern existence that we can see arising another pronounced characteristic of the displacement of vernacular life, the upwelling of a powerful and sustained quest for community.

four

THE QUEST FOR COMMUNITY

"air family: *the false sense of community often found in a conventional office environment.*"

—"Word Watch," *Atlantic*, 1992[1]

"It's been a quiet week in Lake Wobegon." Each Saturday evening, thousands of people in America turn on their radios to hear Garrison Keillor's old-time live variety show, of which the centerpiece is the weekly story about his imaginary hometown of Lake Wobegon, Minnesota. In Lake Wobegon it has *always* been a quiet week, unlike the week just past in the places most listeners live. Although Lake Wobegon serves as a setting for the stories Keillor spins sitting in front of his microphone—a tongue-in-cheek evocation of small-town life—the place still seems very real. We know the various characters, their trials and foibles. We know the old ice fishermen, the guys at the bar in the Side Track Tap, the mothers at home and the dads at work and the kids at band practice. We recognize the Norwegian bachelor farmers. We become intimate observers of a tiny isolated town on the plains where everybody knows everybody else's business. It might be stifling, but it is also snug.

One can learn a great deal about a society at a particular time by looking at its art: its paintings, its music, its plays, and recently its radio and television programs as well. So we might ask ourselves, why is this particular radio program so overwhelmingly popular right now? What chord does it strike in people to inspire such interest and even devotion? One answer, I think, is that it speaks to our deep modern longing to live in a little town such as Lake Wobegon, where everybody knows everybody else (regardless of whether they are on speaking terms with them) and nobody locks their doors. You hear the slap of screen doors behind you as you leave the house rather than the thunk of apartment dead bolts. There is no 911 system, only a volunteer fire department composed of neighbors behaving not unlike the bus driver.

Keillor's *Prairie Home Companion* re-creates a lost entertainment form, the old-time radio show. It conjures up a time when families in actual small towns sat around the big Philco on the living room floor on a Saturday night and listened to songs and stories and news from the glamorous big city. But it is not exactly the same. If you could go back to 1910 and broadcast the "News from Lake Wobegon," would it be popular? I believe it would have been greeted with almost complete disinterest.

People wouldn't have wanted to hear about small-town life in rural America in 1910 because that was the life they lived. Today, when that life is a nostalgic memory in Norman Rockwell prints, people long for small-town community life. We long for it because we need it and we don't have it anymore.

The preoccupation with community that is so much an aspect of current existence is, in fact, a relatively recent historical development. It is a phenomenon so tied to the rise of what I have termed virtual reality that it deserves special exploration. Like the little boy in the removed white environment, people in the modern world seem to feel and act as if something were deeply missing in their lives. What is this missing quality of human existence?

Seymour Sarason named what we are lacking the "psychological sense of community."

> There are times in a society when a myriad of social phenomena indicate that a particular human need is so seriously frustrated, with consequences sufficiently widespread and ominous, as to force us to give it special emphasis. We are living in such times. The young and the old; residents of any geographic area; the more or less educated; the political left, right, and center; the professional and the non-professional; the rich and the poor—within each of these groupings sizable numbers of people feel alone, unwanted, and unneeded. They may spend a large part of their time in densely populated settings, interacting with other people in a transient or sustained way, and yet be plagued by feelings of aloneness and the stabbing knowledge that physical proximity and psychological closeness can be amazingly unrelated.[2]

This lack of a psychological sense of community, and a generalized, often unconscious quest for community, are pervasive characteristics of everyday life today. The word *community* has become ubiquitous. Highway billboards advertise new housing developments as "real communities." Retirement "communities" and nursing homes market to a desire to be a part of community life. Corporations cite the community feeling one will gain by coming to work with them. Titles of articles on community appear with ever-greater frequency on the covers of popular magazines. I have an ad before me that attempts to sell cars by convincing you that you will become part of a community of owners who honk to each other as they pass on the highway if you buy one. Yearning for community seems to have become a modern preoccupation. It is as if everyone were thirsty and always dreamed of water.

It is difficult to tease out and reflect upon an aspect of existence one has always known. For a member of my generation, who entered college in the flowering of the 1960s, who stood in the exciting rain and mud of Woodstock, who lived through the life and death of the communes of the 1970s, thirst for community has always been a part of life. A generation that entered the world at the time of the publication of B. F. Skinner's utopian novel *Walden II* has always had the idea of community as a dominant and motivating influence, whether it has appeared as a national movement to start communes together in the country or as ads aimed at arousing our desire to purchase automobiles. In each decade, however manifested, the dream has been a constant. What do these dreams of community signify?

The Quest for Community

In 1953 sociologist Robert A. Nisbet posed a fascinating answer to this question in his book *The Quest for Community: A Study in the Ethics of Order and Freedom.*[3] Although it is not possible to do justice to this remarkable work in brief form, a few of his key ideas may cast some light on this issue.

In Chapter 1 I proposed the image of a beehive to stand for the organic movement of people organizing themselves in informal or vernacular life. If we were to speak in sociological terms, we could describe cells of the beehive with the term *mediating structures*. Mediating structures are those social groups that stand, or mediate, between large entities like national governments on the one hand and autonomous individuals on the other.

Originally embedded in kinship and locality, these structures—such as extended families, churches, voluntary associations, village governments, and a rainbow of related entities—have for most of human existence formed the primary units in which one dwelled, pursued one's life, and was known.[4] Stable cultures, Nisbet says, must always contain "functionally significant and psychologically meaningful groups and associations lying intermediate to the individual and the larger values and purposes of his society."[5]

Another way of saying that vernacular existence is being displaced is to say that mediating structures are being dissolved as if by a potent social solvent. These associational groups, which provide the bonds that tie individual to individual, are rapidly disappearing. If one looks at the virtual reality of the travel world I described in Chapter 3, for instance, one would find almost no mediating structures. The environment has been sterilized. The people in it are individuals whose interactions are structured by various bureaucratic systems. Autonomous individuals are, Nisbet says, something historically new, members of what can be called "the masses":

> What is crucial in the formation of the masses is the atomization of all social and cultural relationships within which human beings gain their normal sense of membership in society. The mass is an aggregate of individuals who are insecure, basically lonely, and ground down, either through decree or historical circumstance, into mere particles of social dust.[6]

The quest for community that is such a characteristic of modern life is, to Nisbet, an ominous symptom of "profound dislocations in the primary associative areas of society."[7] With its mediating structures gone, its atomized individuals are filled with yearning. What these creatures yearn for is that psychological sense of community that until recently had always been as immediate as the soil beneath one's feet. Such yearning individuals, Nisbet goes on to say, form potent material for totalitarianism. The quest for community is produced by, and in turn supports, the expansion of the modern state. As the modern state expands, those mediating structures from which a sense of community arises are eliminated. Hungry for community, the masses reach out for the only thing left—the false community of the state. "Totalitarianism is . . . made possible only," Nisbet explains, "through the obliteration of all the intermediate layers of value and association that commonly nourish personality and serve to protect it from external power and caprice."[8]

The French Revolution, which aimed to liberate individual rights from the dead hand of medieval tradition, made all people citizens and outlawed many associational entities that were not elements of the state, just as Stalin did in the great community quest of Marxism and Hitler in Nazism later. Free and equal French citizens were to be joined to their government not by local ties but by representative bureaucratic systems. The state itself was to be the national community; all others were suspect. As we have seen, this did not work out, for national community is a contradiction in terms. Community is a local phenomenon.

We thus find ourselves in a modern quandary. For as social problems increase and associational social glues dissolve, greater demands are put upon national and state governments. With mediating structures gone, government departments are the only thing remaining to which citizens can still relate. These entities respond to need by expanding bureaucratic systems, which in turn take any residual authority from whatever local mechanisms might remain. The local library in my rural town finds its control usurped by state regulations. As social problems become worse, the quest for community increases, and that quest in turn is responded to in increasingly systemic and economic ways. These dynamics, over time, have a compounding effect. The result, under democratic conditions, was foreseen by Tocqueville in 1840:

> After having thus successively taken each member of the community in its powerful grasp and fashioned him at will, the supreme power then extends its arm over the whole community. It covers the surface of society with a network of small, complicated rules, minute and uniform, through which the most original minds and the most energetic characters cannot penetrate, to rise above the crowd. The will of man is not shattered, but softened, bent, and guided; men are seldom forced by it to act, but they are constantly restrained from acting. Such a power does not destroy, but it prevents existence; it does not tyrannize, but it compresses, enervates, extinguishes, and stupifies a people, till each nation is reduced to nothing better than a flock of timid and industrious animals of which the government is the shepherd.[9]

Life Is with People

Faced with a person in need, I have said, we are faced with two courses of response: a personal, informal one arising from the historical ways of one's group or place; the other systemic, following a network of small, complicated rules. The habit of response by systems is our modern reality, and we lament the loss of family bonds and small-town life as we yearn for the sense of community they represented, itself a signal of their disappearance. The displacement of mediating structures constituted the fading of the very organs of society in which care for one another originally emerged. What was a society like that responded to social problems this way, and how did it function?

Recently my car was stolen by two bored, poor teenagers from one of the more hopeless sections of town. I know this, although I never met them. What I met instead was the fairly astonishing complexity of systems one encounters as the victim of a theft. After the thieves had been apprehended following a police chase, I went to a suburban police station to pick up my battered car. There were police forms to file and insurance claims to manage. There was dealing with the repair shop and the insurance estimator. In the meantime, the car thieves were being processed though a much more complicated system. They were booked and transferred to the youth detention center. The probation department was involved. One of the young men was classified as having mental retardation, so the mental retardation case management system was involved. He was a previous offender, and I found myself in the curious position of advocating on his behalf within the mental retardation system to try to keep him from being incarcerated in an adult prison rather than getting help. I learned that he was being raised by a single mother and that he gave her many problems, one of which was hanging out with the wrong crowd, such as kids who steal cars. He and his friend had decided to steal my seven-year-old Oldsmobile with 140,000 miles on it rather than a new BMW.

I received a letter from the mayor regretting that I had been a victim of a crime in his city, and he sent along a booklet of crime-prevention tips. I received periodic computer-generated letters on each young man from the probation department informing me of various stages in their processing. Eventually, the letters stopped. I never found out what happened to the young men. Despite my active attempt to be involved on behalf of one of them, I never saw them personally or learned their fate. I only got a brief glimpse of their faces in the holding cell by leaning around a corner of a police desk and seeing them in the television monitor when no one was looking.

How would a vernacular culture respond to such a situation? Questions like this are answered most illuminatingly by cultural anthropologists, investigators who attempt to study and set down the way cultures actually work. Often we think of cultural anthropology as dealing with obscure tribes in jungles whose experience is very far from our own. But this is not necessarily the case. A particular window into this kind of problem is opened in a fascinating reconstructive study that was done about the vanished life of Eastern European Jews in their small towns, or *shtetls*. The book, by Mark Zborowski and Elizabeth Herzog, is called *Life Is with People: The Culture of the Shtetl*.[10]

Within these Jewish cultures, no one could conceivably have yearned for community. Community was omnipresent. In the *shtetl*, life was always lived *with* people. "To be isolated [was] hideous, pathetic, and dangerous. Only when he has a functioning place in a group [can] a man be happy, 'beautiful,' and safe."[11] "Social justice" required "that every poor, sick, or infirm member of the community must be taken care of, permanently or over a crisis."[12] Community tradition meant that every large wedding included a special table for the poor. "To show that the entertainment is social justice rather than charity," the authors reported, "the bride in her snowy gown must dance with beggars in their dirt and rags."[13] Response to others occurred almost exclusively through complex informal means. This included such things as thefts. One of the anthropologists' sources told a story of one theft:

There was a little boy my age who lived in the shtetl. He was an orphan. . . . Just his father was dead and his mother wasn't a strong woman and she couldn't take care of him very well. They were very poor and I remember how that boy used to walk around in those cold winter nights with torn boots. So he comes to the market on one of these busy days and he goes over to one of the stands where a man is selling these heavy boots that we used to wear in the shtetl. They were called *shtivl*. The man has a small shack which he calls a store and he has dozens of boots hanging from the wall and over the doorway. So the orphan stole a pair of boots. All of a sudden the storekeeper rushes out of the store into the market and starts yelling "a *ganef*, a *ganef*," "a thief, a thief!" And the people start rushing from all sides and the policeman comes and naturally they find the orphan boy who stole the pair of shoes, and the boy doesn't deny it. They return the pair of boots and the policeman is ready to take the boy to jail.

All the Jews stand around and the women weep and cry, "What are we going to do, how can we let the police take away a Jewish boy. . . . And he is an orphan, what will happen to his mother? We have to do something about it," and so on. So one fat market woman, who is selling some sort of beygl, picked up one of her dozen skirts—you know, they wore two or three skirts, one on top of the other to keep warm, and the money was kept in a pocket sewn into the last skirt so nobody should steal it. She takes out some money and offers it to the storekeeper and so on until a collection is taken up and about $2.00 is collected. The policeman puts his hand in the back and the money is slipped into his hand and he lets the boy go. This the policeman always expected. Whenever he is called in to an affair like that he knows that he will be bribed to let the "criminal" go.

When the policeman goes away, then the real fireworks begin. The people start yelling that if the community took care of the boy, he wouldn't have to steal a pair of shoes. But the rich people are all too busy giving money to those who don't really need it instead of taking care of the orphans and the widows. So a committee goes to speak to the big shots in the community. And the *gabai* [synagogue trustee] begins to apologize that he didn't know that the widow was so poor and if somebody had only told him he would have seen to it that she and her family had enough to eat and to wear. And, from that incident, the boy was always decked out in good clothes, and they always had food in the house.[14]

The anthropologists here have given us a really rather beautiful example of how an act deemed to be criminal by another society could be responded to in a completely informal, nonsystemic way. This is hard to imagine in our present world. Yet we know such a world existed, even if the *shtetl* might be an extreme example. These studies give us examples of the way vernacular cultures actually handled social problems, as contrasted with the way we do. If we wished to do a little mental experiment, we might recall the woman about to jump off the bridge. Let us transpose her to the heart of the *shtetl*. How would everyone have responded? Would ambulances or their equivalent have been called? Whatever happened, we can safely assume there would have been a bridge full of people, family members sent for, the rabbi on his way, and much wailing and talking and arguing about what to do. And this ignores the point that a member of such a community would be very unlikely to find herself on such a bridge in the first place.[15]

I must explicitly mention a great danger about thinking of the vernacular world as a wonderfully romantic place where everybody looked out for each other and nobody suffered from neglect or even abuse. We know this is simply not the case. Romanticizing the idea of community, in fact, is only another manifestation of the yearning for community. One idealizes in memory what one has lost. Yet one must look to the evidence to see what has been forgotten in the world of systems and individual rights: that stable and functioning cultures did, in fact, have many ways of responding to people that were local, habitual, and personal. For example, in the ancient traditions surrounding the maintenance of the farmers' irrigation ditches, or *acequinas,* in New Mexico, blind people or their surviving spouses could irrigate three acres free of charge without contributing to the community shovel work.[16] Such examples abound.

There is, it is clear, a spirit about the relationship of one person to another that has been lost in the displacement of the associational organs of society by the machinery of caring systems. This spirit might be called by the old name *hospitality*. If we want to understand why formal systems arose and displaced ancient informal associational habits, we have to study the history of hospitality.

five

THE HISTORY OF HOSPITALITY

The man said to Jesus, "And who is my neighbor?" Jesus replied, "A man was once on his way down from Jerusalem to Jericho and fell into the hands of brigands; they took all he had, beat him and then made off, leaving him half dead. Now a priest happened to be traveling down the same road, but when he saw the man, he passed by on the other side. In the same way a Levite who came to the place saw him, and passed by on the other side. But a Samaritan traveler who came upon him was moved with compassion when he saw him. He went up and bandaged his wounds, pouring oil and wine on them. He then lifted him on to his own mount, carried him to the inn and looked after him. Next day, he took out two denarii and handed them to the innkeeper. 'Look after him,' he said, 'and on my way back I will make good any extra expense you have.' Which of these three, do you think, proved himself a neighbor to the man who fell into the brigands' hands?" "The one who took pity on him," he replied. Jesus said to him, "Go, and do the same yourself."

—Luke 10:29-37

I have said that much of my work has involved supporting and encouraging the work of "askers," people who ask ordinary citizens to befriend people with disabilities. The story of Nancy in Chapter 1 is about such a person and someone who asked on her behalf.

Askers go about their work in a variety of different ways. Some go about it very directly, rather like matchmakers, setting out to look for the perfect person to find for the individual they have in mind. Others try to find the perfect associational group, or "mediating structure," like Nancy's church. Still others specialize in isolated children and use creative arts groups, YMCAs, or even putting on a musical together as ways of finding real friendship for children who may otherwise never know it.

Although askers' approaches are diverse, their goals are the same. Askers find a person who is surrounded only by services and watch for people coming down the road who might respond to this particular person who is injured and lying by the roadside. They look for someone to touch the little boy in white. Looking for Good Samaritans, you could say, is their calling.

But how does the vocation of the asker fit into the parable of the Good Samaritan? What happens to the story if you put an asker on that road, and the asker goes up to the priest and the Levite and finally the Samaritan on behalf of the man in the ditch? For that is what we askers do.

Inserted into the parable, the idea is foreign, shocking. It would have made no sense at all for Jesus to have told the story that way. Yet what askers are doing seems to make clear common sense now, in the world of today. How can this be?[1]

The answer, I believe, is this: The road the Samaritan walked down and the road modern askers walk down are not the same road. The dusty roads people walked down in the time of Jesus and the modern superhighways stretching from suburb to suburb are almost completely different from each other. The road the Samaritan walked down simply does not exist anymore, either materially or metaphorically.

It is very important to understand the road we are now walking down. The reason inserting a phrase like "the *asker* went up to the Levite and asked him, 'Would you care for this man and bind his wounds?'" seems so jarring is that the asker has no place on *that* road, that road in the desert, that road in the totally vernacular world. The asker has a place only on the modern road, a road bordered with institutions, professionals, and human service systems. The asker has a place only on a road lined with flowcharts.

Because the injured man in the modern ditch is surrounded by service systems and professionals, any potential Samaritan who may be walking (or driving) down the road today is very unlikely to see the person at all. The wounded man is invisible. He is surrounded by people in white coats.

The asker reacts to this situation by trying to part the crowd of professionals surrounding the person at least a crack. He or she takes the potential Samaritan over to the institutions at the roadside and urges him to peer through the window of the nursing home or homeless shelter or social service program to get a glimpse of the injured man's face. The asker says to the potential Samaritan, "See, this is a person here, just like you." And when the Samaritan asks—"But what do I know about injured people? There are all of these doctors and nurses and social workers who know how to care for people like this!"—the asker persists in parting the professional curtain of belief until the Samaritan can, sometimes, see that he or she and the injured person indeed have a connection.

In fact, there *is* something the Samaritan can do; his place as a brother to the man in the ditch has not been taken over entirely by those hired to care. The asker must do this because today's highways are bordered, metaphorically and sometimes literally, with an unbroken facade of contiguous institutions behind which the faces of the injured can no longer be seen. Or even if they can be glimpsed behind the windows, we know they are not our business. We lack the qualifications.

The asker, in responding to this historically different situation, is trying to rediscover the surface of that original road down which the Samaritan walked. When one sees a homeless man sleeping in the alley across from one's house, one can take him a sandwich and give him a place to sleep or take him around the corner and purchase inexpensive lodging for him for a week. One does not *have* to call the police to take him to a shelter.

What might we call the impulse to respond to this stranger, to take him in? Illich proposes that the word is hospitality. In understanding the history of hospitality, he believes, one can begin to discover what happened to transform the vernacular world of ancient roads, upon which one's feet measured out journeys, into the virtual reality of today's "air travel tube." Posed in another way, where did the "whiteness" the little boy was so afraid of come from? Trying to penetrate and summarize Illich's complex scholarship is a challenging undertaking. Yet it may not do too much violence to his work on this subject to try to illustrate briefly the main thread of his thought.

The Roots of Hospitality

Dependence of the stranger on hospitable reception in the desert is unconditional in a way almost unknown where the land is green.

—Ivan Illich

Hospitality today is considered a minor, if pleasant, social convention. One hosts a cocktail party or exchanges invitations for dinner. One invites a friend to stay overnight. Yet this is far from the original sense of the term.

In its original sense, consider that you are a stranger walking across the desert. Without food and water you will die. After many days' journey, you see ahead the tents of a nomadic tribe. Will the leader welcome you in or drive you off or kill you as hostile? Ancient traditions of hospitality guide the outcome. "Among true nomads such as the Ruwala beduins," Illich noted, "hospitality . . . is still acquired by touching a tentpost, or a child belonging to the host. Breaking bread with the host entitles the stranger to absolute protection, at least for the three days that the food is conceived as staying within his body."[2]

You walk into the camp and touch the tent post. The ancient ritual of hospitality is set in motion, and you do not perish in the desert.

One can find examples of hospitality traditions in virtually all premodern cultures. In a Jewish *shtetl* like that in which a poor boy stole boots, it was a custom that any stranger who appeared at the synagogue on Friday evening would be invited home by someone at the end of the service. First rights to offer hospitality usually went to the prosperous.[3]

Vernacular cultures, in other words, were characterized by set traditions in which hospitality was offered. This hospitality was extended to a degree atypical in our world in which travelers stay in hotels and ill people go to hospitals. Hospitality, however, was precise and specific. People lived in a world in which there were no institutions of hospitality but also in which they claimed no universal relationship with each other. You could not appear, in need, at someone's threshold and think you might be taken in because "all men are brothers." Such an idea simply didn't exist. These facts, Illich believes, are intimately connected.

Let me try to explain this somewhat difficult point. A few years ago I read a line Illich had written that I didn't grasp at first but that clearly seemed key: "I believe the ethos that has led into the managed welfare of our professional service society can be understood historically only as the transmogrification of the Christian vocation to universal fraternity."[4] To understand this point, I eventually began to see, one could start with the parable of the Good Samaritan.

As a resident of this Christian era, I grew up with the certainty that, to capture an approximate phrasing, "all men [and women] are brothers [and sisters]." But this was emphatically not the belief of people at the time the parable was told. People were bound to each other solely through clan or blood relation or perhaps by inhabiting the same city. Other people were simply not of the same category. That is why the parable sounded so completely different to them than it does to us. To Jesus' audience, this story was astonishing. To think that you would pick up someone in a ditch, a stranger, even a hereditary enemy, because he was somehow your *brother*—this idea was crazy! Who was he to you?

To illustrate how differently the world may have been experienced in this way in a society not yet touched by Christianity, the Melanesians of the South Pacific Islands contribute a particularly striking example. The Melanesians, an observer wrote,

> Did not have any organization larger than a village, nor did they have any conception of themselves as a major race. When a Melanesian encountered someone not of his group, although he denoted a likeness, he did not think "it is a man." The word "man" applied solely to his own group, or tribe. Between his own tribe and others he made an enlarged distinction, much as he would between a pig, a bird or a fish, or between himself and any of these animals. The concept of mankind was absent.[5]

This example is relevant because it dramatizes the reality of a culture in which our accepted belief in universal fraternity is absent. This extreme was not, apparently, the world into which the words of the parable were spoken. Yet they help to conjure up the possibility of how different from ours that world really was. "The New Testament," Illich states, "announces a previously unthinkable kind of brotherhood."[6] That idea of brotherhood, he believes, paradoxically set the stage for developments in which hospitality somehow turned into its opposite. One can see the isolated person with mental retardation, abandoned in the depths of the most horrible state institution, as a perversion of the Christian idea of the brotherhood of man, of the concept of hospitality somehow gone terribly wrong.

The Development of Institutionalized "Hospitality"

The Christian impetus to heal the wounds of one's brothers and sisters—who were the hidden Christ in stranger's garb—was transformed into the first benevolent caring institutions. The first of these were called *xenodochia*, created in the fourth century as separate houses that offered hospitality in the name of the community at large. Rather than taking strangers into individual homes, they could now be sent to a specialized place under the direction of a guestmaster. This development disembedded hospitality from the household and, for the first time in the West, delegated it to a shelter or agency that specialized in its practice. This change in the way people welcomed a person in need had enormous effects. "It seems clear to me," Illich once said in a lecture, "that in those societies which then sought to provide such public shelters for 'care,' the previously universal human practice of hospitality withered."[7] That is, individuals no longer had to bother themselves with personally offering the stranger a place to stay. An institution would relieve him or her of this obligation to provide charity, to love.

In that same talk, Illich went on to dramatize the change that took place by repeating this story:

> An experience related by the late Cardinal Jean Danielou simply captures this complex historical truth. A Chinese friend of his, after becoming a Christian, made a pilgrimage from Peking to Rome on foot. In central Asia, he regularly found hospitality. As he got into the Slavonic nations, he was occasionally welcomed into someone's house. But when he arrived among the people of the western churches, he had to seek shelter in the poorhouse, since the doors of homes were closed to strangers and pilgrims.[8]

Yet the personal offering of hospitality was central to the Christian message. At about the same time, John Chrysostom, patriarch of Constantinople (398–407), reminded eastern Christians that hospitality was a personal act and why:

> The smaller the brother is who knocks at your door, the more that you can be certain of being in the presence of Christ. When one receives an important personage, one often does it in the search of vain glory. Thus, it is easy to have a poor intention. But if the guest is an obscure person, one must see Christ. Each in his house should have a space reserved for the outsider: sack, bread, and candle. When soldiers come, you are used to take them in . . . simply because they protect us fighting our this-worldly enemies. And, barely believable, when plain strangers arrive, you have no space!
>
> Have homes in which Christ finds hospitality. Point to the spot and say: this is the place reserved for him as brother. No matter how humble, he will not refuse it.[9]

The word *hospitality*, as Illich has pointed out, was in this text so completely synonymous with the Greek word for "humanity" or "humanness" that the two were used interchangeably by scribes. To offer hospitality was to be human; to be human was to offer hospitality to the stranger. For the believer, the action brought him or her into immediate contact with Christ. But the general practice of receiving the stranger continued to become more disembedded and more specialized.

One of the first "diagnostically" specific agencies appeared in 1095: the Canons Regular of St. Anthony of Vienne. This order not only specified that hospitality for the sick was the purpose of its establishments but also ruled in its charter that care was to be limited to those "touched or mutilated by the fire of St. Anthony."[10] The fire of Saint Anthony, gangrenous ergotism, was a frequent malady among people who ate bread made from rye infected with the fungus Claviceps, which produces a number of alcaloids including lysergic acid, or LSD. Those afflicted by the fire feel "an itching and tingling of the skin, loss of cutaneous sensations, deafness and horrifying visions."[11] Applicants for admission were given a specific examination to be sure they fit the "admissions criteria" specified in the charter. It is curious to reflect upon the fact that whereas we are accustomed to the modern feature of health or social service programs that serve only people with a specific diagnostic label and that routinely use admissions criteria and diagnostic testing to authorize admission, we can look deep into the past and find an example of this currently accepted tenet of established practice.

As historical development went on, through the birth of the hospital in the twelfth century and into the explosive growth of social services in our own era, the certainty that institutionalized compassion was the obvious answer to human problems became more fixed. As Illich has noted, specifically in relation to the birth of the hospital:

> I believe that this social creation of a new institutional device, motivated by heroic charity and deep trust in divine vocation, in the course of the next half millennium was to transform our perception of what a good society ought to be. We can no longer imagine a good society which would lack such special institutional agencies where people with special physical or mental incapacities can be bedded, stored, and treated. The need for hospitalization has become one of our basic certainties, and with it we accept as obvious that there are certain acts of charity which "just cannot be absolved by simple hospitality."[12]

When I reflect on the certainty that modern care—transformed from what was once hospitality—is offered by systems, a somewhat funny image comes to mind. It is as if somebody woke up around the fourth century and said, "Hey—we have all of these people lying in ditches! Didn't you realize that they are our brothers and sisters? We have to figure out how to take care of them somehow!" So the people got organized and built some shelters—in their compassion—to house all of these strangers, hired a bunch of Samaritans to take care of them, and levied some taxes to support the thing.

This, and all of the succeeding efforts over the centuries, offered great benefit to the afflicted. But if we want to find out why the practice of hospitality withered, why potential Samaritans would eventually walk down a highway flanked by institutions, why there is now something that can call itself—without irony—the "hospitality industry," why poor people can live out their lives in the modern dungeons of some public mental hospitals, then perhaps more of an explanation is needed. The original Christian inspiration to "give a hand," to care for my brother, is based on a calling, a *vocatio*. Each person is free to respond, as each is free to love. Illich's research suggests that church authorities at the time of Chrysostom first began to distrust the efficacy of this gift or grace. One had to ensure, through a formal institution, that a stranger, a person in need, would be taken up and cared for. One could not depend on the power of the Spirit to move individuals. Some refer to this as the cooling off of charity, the freezing out of love. If this had not happened, as I have noted here, there would be no place for askers on the modern road.

The World of Formal Systems

In this chapter we have looked at Illich's specific work on the history of hospitality. But another question needs to be asked at this point. I noted in Chapter 1 that we have come to live in a world dominated by the idea of the flowchart, that much of modern life is organized as a formal system. The action of hospitality, however, is only one, albeit an important, aspect of informal or vernacular life now transformed through the application of a systemic view. I used the illustration of a library, an institution that does not arise from traditions of hospitality, as an example of another kind of enterprise. Thus we have to ask, how did this larger idea of systems producing results, be they care or education or healing, come to be dominant?

The answer Illich proposes is surprising. He traces the very beginning of the idea to another fact that we today find unremarkable: that the church should administer such things as sacraments, ceremonies in which one is baptized or married or prepared for death. He explains it like this:

> I have a suspicion that the concept of the tool and the theological concept of the sacrament are intimately related. In fact, Hugh of St. Victor, the first theoretician of mechanical science in *De Sciencia Mechanica*, was also the first one who clearly spelled out the idea of the seven sacraments. Out of the hundreds and thousands of carefully formalized blessings and priestly curses of the devil and such things he picked out seven which, he said, did some-

thing totally different than the other blessings. Less than a hundred years later, at the Fourth Lateran Council in 1215, [the seven sacraments] became a dogma of the Church. I believe that there is a relation between the idea of a tool, which does what you want it to do, and a sacrament, which is a sign God allows men to place but which does what God wants it to do, more or less independently from the power, the intention, or even the decency of the priest who administers it.[13]

This philosophical understanding of a theological fact, the gift of grace, introduces into western thought a specific notion of instrumentality. And it is *this* meaning of instrumental causality that influences the idea and creation of tools. These range from the telescope—to increase the range of the eye— to the hospital—to include more and more clients. Just as some have believed that sacraments take on a mechanical efficiency, others have attributed magical powers to institutional tools. One can sometimes see that the social instrument eventually takes on a life of its own, thus becoming the end.[14]

A line can be traced from this ecclesiastical procedure to the organizational and architectural instruments of the Willard Asylum discussed in Chapter 1. They are expressions of the belief that bricks or personnel procedures will heal. In the asylum and its programmatic heirs, we find the legacy not only of hospitality disembedded from human household and personal act but also of hospitality systematized.

What we see in the "virtual reality" of the modern world, Illich's argument suggests, is an inversion in which the good introduced by Christian revelation is closely related to something far more destructive than that which existed before. He repeatedly uses the ancient Latin phrase *corruptio optimi quae est pessima*, that the corruption of the best is the worst. Illich's friend and collaborator Lee Hoinacki summarizes this message in discussing Illich's view of western society's distinctive character.

There is a kind of alternating rhythmic tension running through it, although today the tension is deeply buried, hardly discernable at all. The rhythm began through a historical insertion, the appearance of a personal *vocatio*, a singular invitation directed to each individual. But men then attempted to turn this into Christianity, Christendom even. Over the years, more rapidly after Constantine's Edict of Milan in 313, the transformation took the shape of what is today called an institution. Men, for various reasons and motives, judged that the call was too ephemeral, too limited, too undependable. It had to be clarified, universalized, regularized. People had to be taught, cared for, engineered. These formal projects, taken together, constitute the presence of evil in the world today. And just as the original appearance was mysterious, transcendental, so the historical result. One is bewildered, speechless, before the horror of the perversion.[15]

By such a path, according to Illich, we have been brought to the existence in which we find ourselves today. As the dominance of systems and professional specialization joined the rise of market economics described by Polanyi, a war against vernacular life arose that continues at an escalating pace. These interlocked forces cut with ever-increasing speed through the fabric of community and culture, just as, in the depiction of John McKnight, the new steel plow invented by John Deere cut the sod of the Great Plains and made a dust bowl of what was once a sea of grass.

In this modern world, the asker pursues his or her seemingly contrary vocation. In the face of caring institutions, askers try to have none; in the face of specialized service tools, all they do is walk down the road and ask. When they see someone in the ditch, they do exactly the opposite of what was done by the originators of institutionalized hospitality in the fourth century. They do not build a shelter and create a service. They do not even undertake to offer ongoing hospitality to a steady stream of the injured, a task that would quickly expand to demand creation of a formalized service. Rather, when they come upon strangers in the ditch they lean over them, learn their names, and try to make them comfortable for the moment. Then they wave their arms and point to the person lying out of sight, usually within institutional confines, and try to call over the next person coming down the road who might be the one person to open his or her heart or even his or her home to this particular neighbor. For the askers, this seems to be the most important thing to do in this age.

I have begun to wonder if in the practice of asking, you are softly singing an old cradle song, the kind of song most people heard their mothers croon to them when they were infants. Somewhere deep inside, this experience is faintly remembered and brings a smile, a subtle response. "A man was once on his way down from Jerusalem to Jericho and fell into the hands of brigands." Responding to the resonance of that old song, deep within the heart, perhaps for an instant people shake off the modern certainty that we lack the qualifications to love and care for each other.

A young football player breaks his neck and is paralyzed. From one moment to the next, he moves from the center of college to the hospital and then to a sterile room in a nursing home. Because of his severe injury, he has disappeared behind medical walls. A local asker hears of him and looks until he finds a local policeman, who befriends the young man and his family. He starts to bring the young man's former teammates and friends into the nursing home and back into the young man's life. In suggesting to the policeman that he might venture into the dense formal service world of the nursing home to help the young man, the asker is not suggesting a new idea but is merely trying to reawaken ancient traditions of hospitality that lie within everyone's breast.

Having closely observed the work of askers, I know hospitality can be reawakened. But this leads to another question: *Must* it be reawakened for it to appear? Can remnants of the informal world, of hospitality, be found surrounding us without such intervention? Curious about this question, I look out of my window onto the street below.

six

DO REMNANTS OF
HOSPITALITY REMAIN?

When our spouse or child, friend or neighbor is in need or trouble, we do not deal with them by means of a computer, for we know that, with them, we must not think without feeling. We do not help them by sending a machine, for we know that, with them, a machine cannot represent us. We know that, when they need us, we must go and offer ourselves, body and mind, as we are.

—Wendell Berry

It is seven o'clock. I lie in my bed and listen to the bells in the cathedral tower, the bells that call me to get up. The bells are the way our little neighborhood, the neighborhood surrounding the cathedral, knows it is morning. In a world in which the prevalent noises are sirens rushing up and down Main Street and trucks and television and pressurized rap music vibrating the windows of passing cars, I think of my great fortune to live in a place where the sound of church bells still marks the rhythm of everyday life; where on Sundays the special chimes for the service still call people to prayer, signaling the time to walk out of their doors and around the corner to the church.

I have been waiting for the bells since the singing lady went by. She walks up the street on her way to morning Mass, singing "la-di-la-la" at the top of a high voice that comes right through the windows. You see her wandering around town and eating over at the corner diner. She had a head injury when she was a child, a neighbor told me. I have become used to listening for her singing, right before the bells. If I didn't hear her for a few days, I would worry about her and ask my neighbor if she was all right.

I lift up the window blind and look at the sky. It is clear today. I wonder if it is cold. I glance over at the flat roof of the school entrance across the narrow street, where the water puddles and the birds drink. It is frozen over. The roof puddle is our thermometer. It has two readings: above and below freezing. It's as much as you need to know to get dressed for work. I pull my wool slacks and a blazer off a hanger.

Walking out the door and down the few steps to the street, I wave to the sister in her classroom who is setting up for the morning; the children have not yet arrived. I pass by the school and the cathedral, taking my regular route, cutting through the tiny memorial rose garden behind the Methodist church. The garden is always immaculately tended, although only dwarf evergreens and a holly can be seen in this season. I swing the iron gate shut behind me. In another block I am at the broad steps of my office building.

The little neighborhood in which I live is in the shadow of the capitol, a part of town most people pass through on the way to doing business there but that they probably don't think of as having a life of its own when the government business day is over and everyone is gone. Tomorrow the streets will be briefly filled for the governor's inauguration, but he and the television trucks will soon be gone and the reviewing stands taken down. Then only the quiet streets will be left, and the sound of the bells can be heard again.

We live in a little row house. In front are the narrow street and a school. If you are home at lunchtime, you can see the children spill out into the street for their noon recess. Two children run out carrying orange traffic cones first and put them at each end of the block to make it into a playground. They bring out balls, and they jump rope and make lots of noise. At one o'clock the sound of their voices is pierced by the sudden staccato ringing of the electric bell. Everybody rushes for the doors and lines up. The traffic cones are taken in, and a few moments later you can see the students sitting in their classrooms, trying to concentrate on their afternoon lessons.

Behind our house is a courtyard of tiny fenced lawns where all of the houses meet in the back. Two of the houses are convents, which house the nuns who teach in the school and run the Catholic hospital. It's hard to imagine quieter neighbors.

When I first moved there I couldn't figure out something about our lawn: It would be cut, and I hadn't done anything. I would notice it starting to get long, and then I would go away every weekend, and on Monday it would have been mowed. It seemed curious; I had never had a self-cutting lawn. Finally one day I saw my neighbor, who is an influential public official, cutting my lawn with a push mower. It turned out that he had always cut the lawn for our predecessors in the house and for our neighbors and for the convents on the other side of the fence. He had grown up on a farm and liked to do it, his wife told me. One day he showed up with a new mower. The old one had broken, another neighbor told me, so he bought a new one. It struck me that he didn't have a lawn himself.

On summer evenings the backyard is lively because of Jerry, our immediate next-door neighbor. Jerry and his wife moved in a few years ago, just after they were married. He is enthusiastic and energetic and is constantly pounding on the walls with a hammer, renovating their tiny three-room house. Every couple of months he calls us inside to see his progress. Jerry's house is half of the miniature double house his grandmother owns; they connect inside somehow. Jerry wants to live in the country, but he moved in because somebody needed to look after his elderly grandmother. So on summer evenings he and his wife and his grandmother and his grandmother's yappy dog will come out on the little crumbly brick patio while Jerry throws dinner on the gas grill. The smells come in our upstairs bathroom window. Late at night we'll hear him call, "Hey, Jane! HEY, JANE!" trying to stir our across-the-fence neighbor out of her sealed-up house. Eventually she will come out into her backyard with her own yappy dog and hand a piece of chicken over the low fence for Jerry to cook for her, or else Jerry will hand her part of the dinner he has cooked.

Jane has some kind of illness and disappears to a hospital for various lengths of time. She keeps all of the windows shut and all of the blinds down in her house all of the time. She sits out in the backyard with her dog in the summer and reads magazines or has long, loud, and spirited arguments at midnight with Jerry, who seems too full of energy to need much sleep. She sits in a lawn chair and sprays Black Flag every time she sees a bug. On Sunday morning last week I caught Jerry in his backyard straddling the fence to Jane's yard balancing a paper plate filled with scrambled eggs and toast. "HEY JANE!" he yelled and handed the plate through her door. In talking with him I realized this wasn't just summer grilling; he took breakfast and dinner to her every day. That is how she ate, I realized. How, in three years, had I never noticed this before?

Often lately I see Jerry and his buddy Fred in the backyard. Fred uses a wheelchair, and Jerry's sunken patio is completely inaccessible. I haven't figured out how the two of them get the wheelchair down there. They sit there and have dinner, Fred using an old board thrown across the arms of his wheelchair as a table. Jerry runs up to Fred's apartment most mornings to help him get ready for work. It takes Fred a lot less time if he doesn't have to do everything himself, because he doesn't have a lot of strength in his arms or legs. Fred has a computer and a couple of degrees and helps Jerry with his courses at the community college.

It's too cold right now, but when it gets to be summer, Jane, Jerry's grandmother, our other-side neighbor Elaine, and the two dogs will go and sit on the concrete steps of the church office and visit. They call it "the beach." My wife stops sometimes and comes back to tell me the neighborhood gossip.

Around the corner from our block is the corner diner, a typical local diner run by a Greek family. If you have had a hard day, it's the best place to go for the kind of comfort only a local diner can bring: a waitress who knows you (you inquire about her cats), the cooks and the waitress yelling at each other about the orders (hey, any baked left?), and a sure cure for anomie—a hot turkey sandwich with french fries, chicken gravy on the fries (a guaranteed heart stopper). It's the kind of food that takes you back to childhood, that drains all of the blood right out of your head and into your stomach, where it will cause less trouble. And since at least one of the ambulance crews stops most nights for a piece of pie or a turkey sandwich, stethoscopes hung like emblems around their necks and walkie-talkies on the table, I figure that if your heart did stop, it would be as good a place as any for it to happen.

One person you see there all the time is Mrs. Brennan, who has the house next to Jane behind us. Mrs. Brennan is a white-haired, spirited Irish widow who takes care of our lawn-mowing neighbor's children during the day. Since my neighbor and his wife are both lawyers, Mrs. Brennan spends most of her days with their young girls, Suzie and Sharon. Mrs. Brennan's husband died young, and her son—the love of her life—lied about his age to get into the Marines and was killed in Vietnam. So Suzie and Sharon are her family, and she cares for them with unlimited love and patience. Mrs. Brennan eats at the diner three times a day. She's there with both girls for lunch and for dinner too if their mom is out of town and the legislature is in night session. She's raised several generations of kids and knows everything about raising children. Sometimes if we are concerned about something involving our young son, we'll ask her advice. "You know I'm not a pediatrician," she always starts, with a caution obviously learned from long experience, and then she'll tell us the answer.

"Take him out in the fresh air and see if that helps. Bundle him up good, though."

When Mrs. Brennan comes alone to the diner, she sits at the table with Grandma. I don't know what Grandma's name is, but she seems to be some kind of adopted grandmother of the Greek family. I had always assumed she actually was their grandmother until recently. She lives next door in a little apartment behind an old storefront, and every evening she works her way slowly with a walker down the fifty feet to the restaurant for dinner. "How's the new hip, Grandma?" we ask her as she comes by our booth. She tells us how her hip operation went and that her ability to walk is coming back. Grandma and Mrs. Brennan have their dinner and talk with everybody, and then she does her nightly job: taking all of the daily special sheets out of the menus and putting in the next day's sheets. Both she and Mrs. Brennan, although elderly, have work to do.

On most evenings many of the diners are regulars, and we all tend to sit up front if we can, by the open kitchen and counter. Kenny sits there every night, and we say "hi" to him. Kenny has a harder time than many people figuring out complicated things, but he seems to do fine in our neighborhood. He lives a few blocks down the street and works as a janitor in a building a few blocks in the other direction. He goes to the cathedral a lot, and I have even seen him give the morning reading at the service, dressed in suit and tie, reading with the slow carefulness of someone to whom reading does not come easily. He has a place in our neighborhood of home, work, church, and diner; and the diner is at the center, where we all see him and know everything is all right. Kenny is very shy, but this past Christmas I heard the mail slot open and an envelope drop through; as I looked through the window I saw Kenny quickly walking away. He had left a Christmas card. So I knew he was getting over his shyness a bit, after so many two-minute conversations in the diner and on the street.

Some days it seems like a good part of the neighborhood is at the diner in the evening, going out instead of cooking in. They probably observe the same limits for restaurants that I do: anything that I can walk to, and no more than fifteen dollars for two—usually twelve dollars. That's easy to achieve at the corner diner if you order the specials, and coffee refills are free. I ate there often when my wife, Beth, was on a trip to Australia. After a month and a half, she finally returned from a grueling experience that included some medical problems and dealing with unfamiliar doctors far from home. She was exhausted when she stumbled off the plane after the twenty-six-hour flight. That evening I took her arm, and we went to the corner diner. As we walked past the counter and the booths, waitresses, neighbors, and regulars greeted her, "Hey Beth! How was Australia?" That was the first time she smiled and visibly relaxed. I guess it felt as if she were home.

Our friend Joan lives a few blocks away with her three kids, her boyfriend, and Mel, who helps with John and Craig, the two children who have severe disabilities. We met Joan when we were home alone one Christmas season. Christmas is not a time to be alone, for us or anybody, so we called the homeless shelters to see if anyone wanted to come to our house for Christmas dinner. The main shelter said it just needed money or maybe contributed food or someone to help serve; another shelter said everyone had gone except for this lovely family that was temporarily down on its luck. So the family came, and we had a wonderful Christmas with the kids (this was before we had any of our own). Later, Joan and the kids were helped in getting their own place, and they started living there and doing pretty well. They were receiving financial help from the county and some agencies, so they were getting by. But Joan was alone, and she had an incredible amount of work with those three kids, and lifting John's wheelchair up and down the steps was hard on her back. The apartment was the kind of slum dwelling rented exclusively to welfare families. She kept telling me how much she wanted to get out of there and get a real house of their own, but how she could manage to do so was beyond me. Welfare wasn't going to pay a higher amount. There were no housing programs she could get into that looked any better than her current situation.

Then Mel suddenly appeared. One day when I went over to Joan's he was there helping with the kids. At first I thought he must be Joan's boyfriend, but then she got a new boyfriend so I figured it couldn't be that. But there he was, every day, month after month, loving those kids, teaching them, trying to help them learn. He started teaching Craig, who wasn't able to talk, a little sign language. Johnny stopped whining and started to say what he wanted. And Joan had a few moments for herself here and there, even enough to go out and meet a new man.

When I got to know Mel a little better, I got him to talk and led him into telling me why he was there. The story he told me was hard to believe, except that he related it in such a matter-of-fact way. "I was standing at the bus stop one morning on my way to work at the auto parts store, and Joan and her kids were waiting too, and we got to talking," he said. "And riding the bus I realized that I wasn't supposed to be working at an auto parts store, I was supposed to be helping those kids. So I went in and quit and came over here. I just love these guys. I don't know anything about this kind of thing—but isn't Craig doing great? Do you see how Johnny is talking?"

Mel worried over things. He worried about the shabby apartment in which Joan and her family were living and how they were short of money, but he also felt insecure knowing so little about what he was doing. I spoke strongly to reassure him; he was obviously more of an expert than I would ever be, judging from the results he was getting. He lived somewhere in the neighborhood, although what he was living on since he quit his job I couldn't imagine. He was very involved in a fundamentalist Christian church and clearly did what he did out of some sense of religious calling, although he said little about it.

Remnants of Hospitality

Why have I recounted certain aspects of life in my neighborhood in such detail? I have done so to illustrate something I have learned: Remnants of ancient traditions of hospitality can often be found in the fragmented informal life beneath our feet. It took me a long time to realize this. For some time I had been gathering stories of personal and community support for vulnerable people; these stories mostly concerned the work of my friends and associates who are askers. Then as my attention became more focused, I slowly started to notice that I could see exactly the same kind of support out of the window of my house without anyone specifically stimulating it or trying, like askers, to bring it into being. In fact, I began to hear almost unbelievable stories, like that of Joanie and Mel. In the description of my neighborhood, I have tried to be very disciplined, to relate only what I have noticed right here, and to describe these things just as they took place.

If I wanted to put on my professional glasses, I could go back through what I have just told and categorize the various individuals who have some kind of disability. I could say that in the stories are people with mental retardation, muscular dystrophy, cerebral palsy, psychiatric problems, drug dependence, and brain damage or people who are elderly and disabled. All of these labels would be true and, in their place, might be relevant. In the clinic they can be important. But if you put on another kind of glasses, those that help you to see the workings of a "subinstitutional," vernacular world, you start to see all of these subtle mutual relationships in which people with some sort of difficulty are bound together invisibly into the neighborhood. In the informal world, I have never heard anyone referred to by any of these labels.

I am convinced that there is nothing special about my neighborhood. I have begun to realize something similar to what you discover about pond water in sixth-grade science. The water in the pond looks just like the processed water that comes out of the tap. But when you dip a test tube in any pond and look at it under the microscope, you discover a very great difference. The water of the pond is teeming with life. I have come to believe it is the same with neighborhoods and communities. Despite the tremendous assault on vernacular life in the reign of the flowchart, if you look with the right lens you usually find that significant ignored remnants of hospitality still exist.

These remnants or remainders can give us a slight taste of what the vernacular world might have been like before it disappeared. Let me give you another example. Last year I visited a remote island in the Caribbean called Saba. Saba is a volcanic island that was so hard to reach that it remained virtually unchanged until a few decades ago. There are no beaches, and until very recently there were no roads and no harbor. Everything had to be carried on one's back or by donkey up and down the mountainous stone "step roads" winding from village to village. For hundreds of years people had lived there in little cottages surrounded by terraces on which they grew enough food to live. For water, they collected the rain.

The Saba I saw was still an exquisitely beautiful place, although its recent connection with the outside world and with the international economy was strikingly visible, perhaps because the changes were so recent and still relatively limited. There were cars now, so people no longer used the step roads. Food was imported—frozen chicken from North Carolina, beer from Holland, vegetables from various places—so small farms no longer surrounded people's houses. If you looked carefully, you could just make out the tracings of the abandoned terraces that had once covered the hillsides, now overgrown with jungle. Faced with imported food, the long tradition of Saban agriculture had apparently withered.

Karl Polanyi has likened this dramatic change in a society's world through a disembedded economics to an infection. What I saw reminded me of a leaf on the forest floor, slowly being taken over by the threads of some woodland fungus that spread and spread until all that remains is gray mold in the shape of the original leaf. This, I realized, was what had intuitively called me to Saba. For if these changes were indeed an infection of some kind, Saba, by virtue of its long isolation, was one of the places in the West in which one could still see the process in its earliest development because it had begun so recently. The old vernacular world of Saban cultural tradition was so recently past—go back fifty years and it was almost like going back three hundred—that traces could still be found, traces that elsewhere are now long submerged.

Thinking about these things, I started up one of the old tracks, the Crispeen track, with my infant son, Nathan, on my back, up through a notch in the mountains. This was the old step road from the village of Windwardside, where I was staying, to the village of The Bottom far below. As I passed through the bougainvillea and orchids, the ferns and elephant ears, the beeping of the cars on the thread of road below faded away. Birds flitted through the underbrush by the narrow track, and bunches of bananas hung down in the abandoned plantations. I walked on through the jungle, up over rocks and down steep slopes, moving deeper into the heart of the woods.

As I came around a turn into a clearing, suddenly a donkey appeared, tied with a rope. Around him was a lost world. For there in the clearing was the Saban world I had thought was completely gone. Bananas stood in tended clumps. Neatly weeded patches of tanya, a kind of potato, spread their broad leaves against the view of the sea far below. Sweet potato vines twisted in tiny plots terraced between the volcanic rocks. As the path looped around a clump of banana trees, a little cottage with its stone cistern on one side appeared. Pigs snorted noisily from their pen out back. It was, I learned later, an old Saban farm that exemplified the way most Sabans—only a very short time ago—used to live. You could reach it only by a track. Everything had been carried in on someone's head or by donkey.

Passing on through a lower field, we came upon an old black man, machete through his belt, tending sweet potatoes. We chatted for a bit. "This is beautiful," I said finally, impulsively, gesturing around his fields. "In all my walking around in the past few days I haven't seen any farms—only ruins of farms!" The old man agreed. This was one of the only ones left. "Why is this?" I asked him. "Oh," the old man replied, in a deep, almost Jamaican accent, leaning back on a stick, "The young men, they don't want to farm. They wants to work for the cash money so that they can . . ." and he gestured, taking a nip out of a bottle.

When I told the old man that his fields were beautiful, I described them accurately. What I had stumbled upon there in the jungle was a remnant of an agricultural existence I had thought was completely extinct. It was a living remainder of the vernacular culture that had once blanketed the island. And I had seen a patch of it before everything disappeared. I felt as dazzled as a bird-watcher who has just caught a glimpse of a plumage bird considered to be extinct.

It seemed to me as I walked along that as you develop an eye for these cultural remnants, you recognize them more and more easily. Underneath the surface of the modern "cash money" world, the modern system world, here and there fragments of the past still exist, persisting largely unnoticed into the present age.

To get a glimpse of this one exercises, in the words of Margaret Mead, "a capacity to listen to the broken accents of the present, and reconstitute the whole which was the immediate past."[1] It is like looking at fragmentary remnants from which skilled curators are able to reconstruct an ancient fresco, drawing it in between the bits and pieces in light lines to give you a sense of the whole that once was.

The remnants of the vernacular world I was attempting to discern have to do with traditions of hospitality that, with the right eye, can still be found. The way people with various kinds of problems are seamlessly supported in my neighborhood is one kind of remnant. Recently I discovered that these remnants can sometimes leave physical tracings of their existence.

Hobo Signs

Everyone has heard about hoboes, that generation of homeless men who rode the rails during the days of the dust bowl and the Great Depression. What I did not know until recently was that the loosely bound subculture of men leading this lonely and hazardous existence had its own language to indicate both hospitality and danger.

I met a man in his sixties who remembered the hoboes. He told me they were always coming to the back door. His mother, he recalled, fed them and then asked them to do some chore around the place, splitting wood perhaps. Over time he realized that all the hoboes who passed through and had never been there before came to his mother's back door, although they didn't come to the back doors of his friends' houses. So one day he asked his father about it. How did they know to come to his mom's kitchen door? His father, the man told me, led him down to the street. There on the curb were some little marks. He didn't remember, years later, what they were, but I drew them for him. They were probably, I guessed, one or perhaps both of the sketches in Figure 6.1.

Hoboes, like nomads, traveled in a desert in that they had no place of abode. Everything depended upon knowing where they could find hospi-

"Kind-Hearted Woman Lives Here"   "Food Here if You Work"

FIGURE 6.1   Hobo Symbols

tality. They might be hungry, even sick. Picking the wrong house or the wrong town might mean being run off by dogs, put in jail, or even shot. Picking right could mean a free meal, being nursed back to health, even free care from a doctor. Thus, over the years a network of signs, signs that had a long European evolution before being carried to the United States, spread until they virtually blanketed U.S. hobo routes. These indicators of hospitality, although as visible as signposts to those necessarily guided by them, remained—even at their fullest flowering—invisible to most of the inhabitants of the places marked. A few examples of hobo signs, collected in the 1970s before they disappeared, are shown in Figure 6.2.[2]

I have attempted to illustrate in this chapter that just as in the Willard Asylum, a subinstitutional world exists even in the midst of modern western society. Our society is not a single institution but is the combined force of the many interlocking institutions of the modern world and of the virtual reality of the world they generate. In this reality the tracings of cultural traditions of hospitality are as invisible as the tracing of hobo signs on curbstones in the 1930s. Yet like the hobo signs, they are still there for those who can see them.

It is this informal world that those who are askers try to enter and nurture. It is this ignored and eroded but still existent world that makes for the subtle interrelationships described in my neighborhood, relationships too delicate for any systemic device such as a social service agency to ever bring about. In this world, too, lies the origin of the occasionally astonishing, even mysterious event of forming an alliance with strangers—for example, why Mel would quit his job and, for no visible reward, replace the absent father of handicapped children until a new father was found; why in the heart of Nazi Germany many ordinary citizens put their lives at risk to take in and hide Jews;[3] why in Le Chambon an entire village risked deportation and death to become a haven for the hunted and oppressed, led by a remarkable asker, the village pastor.[4]

"A Religious Talk Here Will Get
You a Free Meal"

"You May Sleep in the
Hayloft Here"

"If You Are Sick,
They'll Care for You Here"

"An Ill-Tempered Man
Lives Here. Danger"

"This Is a Good Place
for a Handout"

"A Doctor Lives Here.
He Won't Charge for His Services"

FIGURE 6.2   Hobo Symbols

But it is not the exceptional that is most relevant to a study of hospitality in relation to the problems of living experienced in the modern age. It
is rather the tiny ways in which remaining hospitable traditions persist
even in the midst of the complex systems that make up the world in which
we now exist. It is about finding remnants of certain aspects of culture.
How might efforts to improve existence be predicated upon the relevance
of the informal world, the cultural world, to the current human situation?
How can we approach things with the image of the beehive rather than
the flowchart? How might one understand the informal world through
the use of this word *culture?* Chapter 7 takes up these questions.

seven

STIMULATING CULTURAL HEALING

I seemed to be thinking for myself independently, but I now realize that multitudes of minds were moving in precisely the same direction. . . . I suppose that when a flight of starlings circles in the air, each single bird feels that it is moving in its own initiative.

—H. G. Wells

Everywhere mind flows into mind . . . individuals are not wholly separate from each other but are unconsciously linked together. Like islands of an archipelago, joined together underneath the sea that separates them, we are knit together by invisible and unconscious ties.

—Christopher Bryant

In the late 1960s, psychiatrist Ross Speck made a remarkable discovery. He was training during the day at a notable psychoanalytic institute, learning how to conduct classical psychoanalysis. His background was impressive; his analytic training lineage went back to Freud himself. But in the evenings, without telling anyone at the institute, he started to hold large and startlingly dynamic therapeutic meetings in the homes of families in which a member had been diagnosed as schizophrenic. These "schizophrenic" young adults had received all of the traditional therapies to little effect. As a family therapist, Speck suspected that the schizophrenic roles of many of these people were maintained by the rigid bonds of a symbiotic attachment to their parents. Everyone in the family was suffering greatly from the behavior of the mentally disordered person, but somehow an unconscious conspiracy prevailed to keep things just as they were.[1] Rather than seeing this problem as existing exclusively with the "ill" person, Speck began to believe it was more the case of a family stuck in a "reverberating pathological process." But what could he do—herd the entire extended family into the psychiatric clinic? Instead, he tried something completely new.

When such a family reached the point where it simply couldn't live with a son or daughter another minute and was desperate for something—anything—to be done, Speck told the family members that he would agree to help them if they would invite forty or fifty, even up to seventy, people into their home for an evening. Speck came with a team of associates. He told the assembled crowd, jammed somewhat anxiously and uncomfortably into the family home, that one of the biggest problems of modern life was that people had lost their tribes. For all of history, until the industrial revolution stripped them away, people had lived in tribes. These people tonight were lucky, for they could look around and see who the members of their tribe were. He'd then lead the group in some quick and unexpected exercises. He would have them jump up and down with him and yell "hoo!" or hold hands and sway—anything that would quickly shake up the rigidified structure of the group and help its members to feel like a tribe again. With a series of deft moves, he'd help the group uncover the conflicts and difficulties that were simmering under the surface of the problem.

The group would polarize. Anger would emerge. People might yell or weep or try to flee. (In one case, Speck had to check with a father's physician beforehand to be sure his heart could stand the strain.) The group's energy would build to a crescendo. Then, invariably, the principal thing Speck was looking for would emerge. Activists would come forth *from within the "tribe"* to organize ways of solving the problem. If a son had been "stuck" living with his parents, for instance, such activists would organize others to find him an apartment, get him a job from some friend, physically move him out, or do whatever was required. Often, psychiatric symptoms would fade dramatically.[2] Rather than feeling powerless and handing the "problem" over to professionals, the group would find its own ability to grapple with and resolve seemingly intractable situations or even pathologies. Speck gave this phenomenon a compelling name; he called it *retribalization.*

Speck was convinced that the capacity for retribalization still lingered just beneath the surface of modern life. He believed that if you could intervene in the right way, you could precipitate its reemergence. This usually required the energy of a crisis. The intervener was not a therapist but a catalyst. He or she aimed at catalyzing a "network effect" through which tribal feeling—what Seymour Sarason has called the psychological sense of community[3]—would surface. He or she did this by dropping a big rock into the tribal pond. Only in the most severe crisis would a family invite many relatives, friends, and neighbors to hear intimate details about its family life and to become directly involved in trying to solve problems it had often worked for many years to keep hidden. In these gatherings, no one could successfully hide behind a mask of distance or of an invulnerable social role. Instead, social processes exploded.

"In social network intervention," Speck and colleague Carolyn Attneave wrote,

> We are experimenting with the idea of setting in motion the forces of healing within the living social fabric of people whose distress has led society, and themselves, to label their behavior pathological. . . . So far as we can tell, most people have some contact with at least 40 or 50 people who are willing to be assembled in a crisis. In such an assembly, tribal-like bonds can be created or revived not only to accomplish the tasks of therapeutic intervention for the current crisis, but to sustain and continue the process. . . . The goal of network intervention is to utilize the power of the assembled network rapidly to shake up a rigidified system in order to allow changes to occur that the members of the system, with increased knowledge and insight into their predicaments, would wish to occur—and for which they are responsible.[4]

Finding the Informal World

For psychoanalyst Ross Speck to encounter the phenomenon of retribalization is as unlikely as it was for me to encounter my psychiatric hospital's subinstitutional world of bakers and groundskeepers. Yet somehow events caused both of us to step far enough outside of the certainties of the formal institutional world of psychiatry to encounter the same phenomenon—the informal world lying beneath. This informal world was not the systemic one we were used to but one that might be described by the word *cultural*. Speck's understanding that he was catalyzing a cultural phenomenon was best evidenced by the way he concluded network interventions. When the problem-solving phase of the new tribe was in full swing, he and his associates would fade out the door without saying good-bye, leaving the group hard at work.[5]

Speck was not alone in drawing attention to the inherent healing ca-pacity of cultures, although his dramatization of this essentially anthropo-logical insight was unique. Others within the mental health field at about the same time pointed to evidence of the same phenomenon. Research showed that if you asked ordinary people to whom they turned for help in times of difficulty, they listed ministers, friends, and hairdressers—even bartenders—as the first people to whom they turned for advice.[6] In other words, people always looked for help first in the informal world and last in the formal one, even though most clinical work and public policy seem to be based upon the opposite belief.

In informal worlds there are certain people to whom others turn when they have problems in living. These were the kinds of people I stumbled over in the nonprofessional sector of the mental hospital and who seemed to me to be natural therapists. They include the kinds of problem solvers Speck precipitated to emerge in a group. In any true community, people know exactly who these people are. I have described some who live in my neighborhood. The increased awareness of the presence of such people in society even led psychologist A. E. Bergin to suggest a curious possibility regarding the phenomenon of "spontaneous remission."

In research on psychotherapy, it is well-known that a certain percentage of people who have a problem for which treatment is ordinarily sought improve *whether they get treatment or not*. With depression, for instance, a certain percentage of people seem to recover without help. Since no for-mal help has been given, such recoveries are seen as "spontaneous." In other words, an inherent characteristic of the malady involved seems to be that it sometimes goes away spontaneously. What Bergin proposed is the possibility that these problems may not be going away spontaneously. What may have happened instead is that they encountered healers whom the professions are unable to see. "Is it unreasonable to suppose," he asked, "that people in distress have simply discovered potent change agents as they exist naturally in society, and have put them to work with sufficient impact that they create changes equivalent to [those] appearing in psy-chotherapy?"[7]

Much recent health research has reported findings about how you have fewer illnesses if you don't live alone, if you have a pet, if you volunteer to help others. These studies make some interesting points, all of which are confirmed by the common sense of daily experience. Yet it is testament to the modern belief that care is produced by formal systems that research is undertaken to prove that people fare better if they live in a sense of community with others. As my friend Roger Peters once quipped, perhaps that is why they call it *re-search*.

The Peckham Experiment

Speck catalyzed inherent cultural capacities for healing in modern life through the agency of crisis. What if you set out to help these capacities to emerge on a continuous basis? What if you tried to cultivate a healing culture rather than to build a service program? Certain intentional communities provide examples.

Camphill communities are places where people with mental retardation and similar disabilities live and work together in villagelike settings. These communities are organized around farming or craftswork and follow the suggestions for social living proposed by Austrian philosopher Rudolf Steiner. Everyone lives together in family homes, everyone works together, everyone's efforts contribute to the common good, and no one is paid. One cannot find people who are labeled either staff or clients. There is no agency or "program." There are no organization charts. Yet in these places people with disabilities experience the finest conditions I have seen anywhere in my work with social initiatives. Their well-being arises from the creation of a healthy culture that everyone shares a conscious stake in sustaining.[8]

Intentional communities, for all their importance in demonstrating and sustaining cultural approaches, remain a special case. Very few people choose to live in such alternative settings. Thus, it would be of particular interest if we could find an example of a way in which the healing capacities of an ordinary neighborhood of ordinary people could be enhanced. Such a project was undertaken in the years immediately preceding World War II in a suburb of London. It came to be called the Peckham Experiment.

The Peckham Experiment was born of the visionary thinking of two unusual physicians, G. Scott Williamson and Innes Pearse. The phenomenon they were interested in was the larger issue of health. Everybody noticed that people became ill with various diseases, and physicians then treated them. But in any group of either people or animals, there were always those who did *not* fall ill. So Williamson and Pearse turned the usual question on its head: What *kept* people from succumbing to illness?

Further, they made the great leap of going beyond individual factors to examine the characteristics of a community and to try to do something about individual health by focusing on the strength and viability of the community in which people lived. Although today we might call their emphasis sociological, Williamson and Pearse came to this insight from a biological perspective. They stopped calling themselves physicians, termed themselves *biologists* instead, and founded the Pioneer Health Centre. The center was as unlike a medical clinic as one could possibly envision. Rather, in their explicit image, it was a wax foundation sheet around which community could form.

Instead of erecting medical offices, the two doctors and their group of co-workers put up a building that looked like what today we might call a community center. It had a swimming pool, and a teapot was always on in a cozy corner for mothers of young children who might gather there. There were various kinds of equipment but no program staff. Staff might erect programs or control people—the antithesis of the free formation of community. Architecturally, the building was designed to encourage natural groups to form. To use the center, you had to meet certain requirements. Your entire family had to join with you. Second, you had to live within "pram-pushing distance" of the center. This is how the founders described it:

> The whole building is . . . characterised by a design that invites social contact, allowing equally for the chance meeting and for formal and festive occasions. . . . It is a field for acquaintanceship and for the development of friendships. . . . In these times of disintegrated social and family life in our villages, towns, and still worse in cities, there is no longer any place like this. Nevertheless, man has a long history of such spaces that have met the needs of his social life and the tentative adventure of his children as they grew up: the church, the forum, the market-place, the village green, the courtyard; comfortable protected spaces where every form of fruitful social activity could lodge itself.[9]

As new members came in and spontaneous activities appeared, the beginnings of an informal associational life started to grow. The matrix of the center served as a sort of soil for this culture. Tentative friendships began to form, their initial actions "like the tender root hairs put out by a plant in new soil."[10]

As the culture of the center began to establish itself, Williamson and Pearse served members in a preventative capacity and carefully monitored the health of the population. They showed that their approach could be documented by the improved health of individuals. They began to make a strong case that the social planning that led to the kinds of barren cities in which modern people dwell suffered from specialists who were "unwittingly sterilizing society." Their work began to draw attention. Was there indeed another way of looking at the phenomenon of health other than the prevailing one? At this moment World War II exploded on the British scene, and the experiment was lost, never to be effectively re-created.

Mourning Community Lost

The intervening years since the Peckham Experiment have witnessed, if anything, greater sterilization of the soil in which human culture might take root. In the modern United States, almost no such places of convivial congregation are left, not even places comparable to the traditional English pubs that must have populated the neighborhood around the Pioneer Health Centre. Suburbs are barren dwelling places in which centralized planning, through zoning, has eliminated the possibility of anything resembling a neighborhood tavern or café. Sociologist Ray Oldenburg, author of the delightful *The Great Good Place: Cafés, Coffee Shops, Community Centers, Beauty Parlors, General Stores, Bars, Hangouts, and How They Get You Through the Day,*[11] makes a compelling case for why such places are essential for community to form and how they are being methodically displaced by the kind of "virtual reality" I talked about in Chapter 2. The characterization of airports I made there could apply as well to shopping centers, those totally managed environments in which simulated replacements of the shops of Main Street erect their facades. Through zoning restrictions, Oldenburg once said, community has become illegal.

In these sterilized places, we live the isolated lives of modern men and women, treating our yearning for a sense of community with television and self-help books, "the inspirational literature of people without community,"[12] to seek cures for our many ills. But this, we often hear, is the price we must pay for our modern, mobile lifestyles, for the fact that many people today live not in tribes but in nuclear families. The world has changed, and we have adapted to this new reality. But is this actually so?

When I ran group homes for people with mental retardation, one year something happened to me a few days before Christmas that I still remember well. A young man who had been abandoned at birth by his parents came by the office with his suitcase. "I'm going to see my parents for

Christmas," Carl announced with great determination as he started out the door. My heart stopped. I knew—and I knew that he certainly knew—that he had no parents. Where on earth was he going?

No time of year is more excruciatingly painful than Christmas for those who have lost their families. I had witnessed a lot of such pain over the years. So I knew the pain of abandonment was at the root of what Carl was thinking and feeling and saying. But from long experience with people with mental retardation I knew something else: Such people, when faced with psychological pain, use psychological defense mechanisms to help contain it, the same as anyone else. In people with mental retardation, the defenses they use are frequently simpler, which is one thing that has always attracted me to such people. In the same situation, I would probably have said something like, "It's all right getting along without parents—it's not too bad. I have a lot of things to do over the holiday season." It wouldn't be true, of course, even if I had firmly convinced myself that it *was* true. The fact is that it is a terrible and irremediable loss to be abandoned by one's family. It is such a great loss and so very painful that I very likely wouldn't be able to feel it directly lest I weep uncontrollably from Thanksgiving through New Year's. Carl was more direct. He simply denied that it was true. Later, one of us reached Carl and dissuaded him from wandering off to the bus station.

Our belief in the existence of the nuclear family, Nigerian psychologist Azubike Felix Uzoka has said, *is just such a denial of a loss too painful to be admitted.* The nuclear family, he believes, is not a fact but a myth. When the industrial revolution ripped individuals away from the tribes in which they had lived from the beginning of time, it created a "massive repression, a denial process that emerged as the nuclear family." "This myth," Uzoka goes on to say,

> sought to heal the anguish of separation by denying the very existence of the larger family—the extended family. In doing this, loyalties to the extended family became invisible—largely submerged under the weight of the nuclear mythology. In effect, the concept of the nuclear family is a denial process that was adopted for coping with the problems of alienation emanating from the loss of the supports of the extended family.[13]

Despite the maintenance of our modern mythic belief in the nuclear family, Uzoka believes, convincing evidence shows that people still attempt to function as if they had extended families and, in fact, do continue to exist in them, although this existence may be submerged. Ross Speck's demonstration that one's tribe can be precipitated into visibility and remobilized under conditions of crisis is one confirmation of the reality of this statement. From the perspective of the language I have been using, these are proofs that people continue to exist in some remaining remnants of an informal vernacular world and that they need this world just as much as they did in prehistoric times. Some posit an extended family as the basic organic unit of a culture. This submerged and ignored reality about how people actually live can start to come to life again if a suitable space is made for this inherent tendency of human culture to manifest itself. That space might be a network intervention or an intentional community or a Pioneer Health Centre. The fact that people should do this when the managed space of virtual reality is stripped away from a small space is no more surprising than the fact that grapes ferment if left in a vat. Both are inherent tendencies of life itself.

What Is Culture?

In the preceding paragraph I used the word *culture* to speak about what I have thus far described as an informal or a vernacular world. Since this word can carry so many meanings, let me take a moment to be clear about what I mean when I use it.

The clearest image I can use is the one of grapes. As I am writing these lines it is the first day of the grape harvest in the Finger Lakes region where I sometimes live, and I can hear the grape-harvesting crew working in the vineyards on the hillside above my home. Once those grapes are knocked off the vines by the mechanical harvester and dumped into vats, the winemaker is subject to one natural law: The grapes in that vat *will ferment*. Every winemaker knows there is no trick to making grapes ferment. All grapes will ferment. In fact, if you want to try to keep them from fermenting, you have to either refrigerate them or dose them with chemicals to suppress fermentation. In making wine a winemaker guides the natural process of fermentation in ways he or she would like. To know about this is to know about the culture of grapes and wine.

Human culture, to my mind, is an analogous phenomenon. Cultures are what people create if left to their own devices. Doing so is inherent in their natures. They are culture-building beings as much as honeybees are hive-building beings. Margaret Mead described cultures, in this case the lost culture of the Jewish *shtetl*, this way:

> Human cultures are the most distinctive creations of human beings, drawing
> as they do not only upon the special contributions of the singularly gifted, but

upon the imagination, explicit and implicit, of every man, woman, and child who live within them, and through them, and who, each generation, remodel the traditions which they have received from their cultural ancestors. But although human cultures are the most distinctive creations of the human, they are also the most fragile, for they live primarily in the habituated beings of living persons. Like a dance, for which the music and the choreography have never been written down, a great part of human culture is lost to humanity when the group which has carried it, devotedly, in every word or gesture, is dispersed, or destroyed, or forsakes the traditional ways for ways which are new.[14]

I very much like Mead's image of cultures as distinctive and fragile creations. They are astonishing in their delicate fragility because they exist not of material but, in psychologist John Dollard's image, as an "organismic stream" of new lives funneling in at one end and old, used-up lives funneling out the other. Individuals live, change, and perish, but their common cultural patterns remain, evolving with only slight alterations under the normal course of events. "In order to get this point of view," Dollard suggested, "you have to close your eyes slightly so that the individuals disappear but the connected sense of their habitual life remains."[15]

These "fragile creations," this "sense of habitual life," this culture can, however, be disrupted or displaced. When this happens on a widespread basis, our very ability to live is undermined. For it is our culture that gives basis and meaning to our lives.

This insight prompted Illich to define culture in what I find to be the most useful way. Culture, he has said in a variety of different statements, is that with which we face pain, sickness, and death. In one of his books he defined it at greater length this way: "Each culture was the sum of rules by which the individual came to terms with pain, sickness, and death, interpreted them, and practiced compassion toward others faced by the same threats. Each culture set up the myths, the taboos, and the ethical standards needed to deal with the fragility of life."[16]

When I say that caring for each other is an inherent tendency in society (not the only one, obviously!), this is what I mean: that humans are cultural beings, and support for each other in the face of the fragility of life is in large measure what human culture is all about.

In the modern world we have tended to forget that with which our forebears faced all of the joys and the terrors of life. We have replaced it with the certainty of systems to provide for our needs. We have done this for a number of complex reasons, among which is the idea that care is scarce.[17]

I said that when I was on the island of Saba I saw old, original Saban cottages with rain cisterns to collect water. It was clear that in the entire history of Saba, nobody had ever thought of water as scarce. Saba was simply a place where it sometimes didn't rain very much, and rain was all you had. With the beginnings of development, however, people were hooking up showers and flush toilets and washing machines. Soon there was talk about needing a desalinization plant, because water was changing from rain collected off the roof to a "scarce resource." Soon, the cultural traditions surrounding the construction of distinctive Saban cisterns, patterns for the usage of water, and many other fragile aspects of Saban culture began to disappear, with metered water piped into all of the homes.

What you can witness on Saba with rare clarity is the invention of scarcity, in this case a scarcity of water. Thus, scarcity is not a fact but an assumption. In talking about care, or what I earlier characterized as hospitality toward strangers, we are operating under a parallel assumption. There is a scarcity of hospitality, I believe, exactly as there is a scarcity of water on Saba.[18]

Throughout the foregoing I have tried to argue that hospitality is not scarce but is a part of human culture. It is this culture that is rapidly being submerged. In our formal world, we can perceive suffering only as a call for new programs. Yet at the root this thinking makes the underlying problem steadily worse, as the culture is progressively drowned.

There is a phenomenon in winemaking known as a "stuck fermentation." It is the bane of winemakers, and a good winemaker is needed to correct it. In a stuck fermentation the natural process of fermentation proceeds so far and then stops. Since the inherent tendency of grapes is to ferment, this situation always occurs because something in the must is suppressing the ability of the yeast to work. The winemaker's job is to find out what is causing this suppression and to remove the cause sufficiently to allow the process to begin again. He or she might change the acidity, for instance, and then try to catalyze fermentation back into action with a potent yeast mixture started in the lab.

Retribalization, the Peckham Experiment, my colleagues who ask ordinary citizens to extend the mutuality of care to people with disabilities—all are doing the same thing. All believe that hospitality and mutual care inhere in cultures and that culture, although submerged, still exists. They are trying to restart the "stuck fermentation" of the culture in which we have our being. Each is a demonstration that this perception is correct. Each shows that if we can drop our belief in certain interlocked certainties—the scarcity of care, the myth of the nuclear family, that complex formalized service systems are the response to human need—developments of a completely different and surprising nature are possible. For even under the dominion of virtual reality one's culture sleeps in fragments, ready to reemerge if space can only be made for it to resume its energetic work.

This issue of culture as a basis for activity may not apply exclusively to the world I have called "vernacular." It can be seen in professions and agencies too. I turn my attention to these in Chapter 8.

eight

REMNANTS OF CULTURE IN PROFESSIONAL HEALING

It was ten o'clock on Good Friday evening, and my wife had been in labor for twenty-four hours when Dr. Hall said, "Now we need to do a cesarean." She had seen it coming for some hours and had caught the anesthesiologist in the hall to quietly tell her to check with her before she left for the night; an operation would likely be necessary this evening. She hadn't mentioned it to us yet, though. There was still a chance that the natural processes would work on their own. But by ten she had concluded that for the health of our baby it was wisest to operate. They wheeled Beth into the operating room and handed me a scrub suit to put on.

The small operating room, bustling with doctors and nurses, suddenly swung into activity in this hidden area in the heart of the sleeping hospital. Dr. Fairweather, the anesthesiologist, showed me where to sit next to Beth's head and put my hand into Beth's where hers showed between gaps in the surgical drapes. Dr. Hall was working rapidly, talking to the obstetrical resident, giving instructions to the surgical nurse. The pediatric nurse practitioner readied the scales and blankets for the baby. She came around behind us and whispered, "Now when the baby comes out, I am going to walk it over to that table and scale to check it over before I bring it back to you. I want you to know this so you won't think anything is wrong when I do it." How very thoughtful that small gesture seemed to me—for when it actually took place, we would have been greatly alarmed when they took our baby over in that corner where we could not see. So Dr. Hall worked, and we waited. I held Beth's hand. We waited to see if we would have a son or a daughter. Only Dr. Hall knew from the tests. Dr. Fairweather asked us the names we had chosen for each possibility. I think perhaps Dr. Hall had shared the secret with her.

Then suddenly the nurse was bustling a bundle behind us, and there was a cry from within her arms. "I understand that this little baby's name is Nathan," she called to us joyfully. "And he is just fine." In a moment Nathan was with us, and Dr. Fairweather tucked him into the crook of Beth's neck as Beth lay immobilized on the table. Dr. Fairweather took my arm and set my hand on top of Nathan, holding him snugly against Beth as Dr. Hall sewed Beth up.

They took Nathan to the nursery for a checkup and wheeled Beth to a recovery room. She lay there, weary but happy, while Dr. Hall did all of the postsurgery paperwork somewhere. It was now close to midnight. Except for a short night's sleep, Dr. Hall had been with us continuously since the evening before. She was tired and had worked despite having the flu. She had canceled all of her office appointments and had sat in the room talking to Beth, not rushing anything, for most of that time. It was known in the hospital, we learned, that this was the way Dr. Hall did deliveries, just as it was known that Dr. Fairweather always insisted that new babies be brought immediately to the mother and father in the operating room, just as Sarah—Beth's labor and delivery nurse—came early and stayed late because she was our Lamaze instructor and took a special personal interest in us as members of her group.

Finally, Dr. Hall came in. Despite the late hour and being ill, she looked refreshed. She smiled at Beth. Then she reached into the pocket of her white coat and pulled out a little pink-and-blue box containing a silver baby spoon. She laid the box on Beth's stomach. "Let me be the first to congratulate you," she said softly. Then she went home to her own bed.

I tell you this personal story for a specific reason. In this book I have contrasted again and again the neglected virtues of the informal, vernacular world with the limitations of the formal, professional, and systemic one. Yet here we were in the midst of the pinnacle of professional caring— the modern hospital and the surgical suite. We were surrounded by systems and advanced technology. We were in a world of white coats and beeping electronic machines. Yet in that world we had been embraced by love and by care.

How can we understand this apparent contradiction of everything I have said up to this point? Let me reply in this way. We have all heard many stories about hospital births that are the opposite of the story I just told. Many mothers have complained about having labor induced rapidly so the obstetrician could make it to a golf date, about having drugs given for normal births even if one objected, about being treated as objects. The mothers' movement that promotes midwifery and home births came out of a reaction to the experience of being processed for birth as if through the cogs of a machine.

Beth's and my experience pointed out something I knew but have not yet said here: that professional caring and compassion can exist even in the most formal settings. But it would be an error to believe that such examples are the norm. Rather, the counterproductivity of medical systems and settings is the norm today. Faced with this reality, one comes to accept that the old Norman Rockwell ideal of a doctor is a thing of the past, as is the nurse with time to get to know the patient, as is the informality of the caring hospital. Yet Dr. Hall works alone, day and night, 365 days a year; is there for every delivery; and seems never to take a vacation—just like the village doctor in my grandparents' time. Beth's nurse sat and talked with her and plumped up her pillows, just as nurses used to do when nursing was less rushed. When Nathan was wheeled in from the nursery on Easter Sunday, he (and all the other babies) had construction-paper rabbit ears that had been taped on the tops of their bassinets by a lady from the women's auxiliary. It was like a memory from another time. This, I believe, is exactly what it was.

The Consequences of Imbalance

One of the greatest temptations that arises from drawing a contrast between the formal and informal helping worlds as I have been doing is to conclude that the former is all bad and the latter is all good. This is not true. It is the severely skewed balance between the two that produces such negative effects. Our modern world, as I have pointed out, is so dominated by formal systemic approaches that informal ones have been almost totally forgotten. Cultural remnants, however, continue to exist and can be seen by those who have developed the eyes to do so. These remnants, like the remote farm on the island of Saba or the ways people help those with disabilities in my neighborhood, are fragments of cultures that once blanketed the world. Such fragments can remain even within the caring professions. I had encountered such a remnant at the birth of our son.

As professions have risen in dominance, they have assumed authority for aspects of life that the ordinary rules of one's culture once governed. This growth has led to our modern world in which you require one certified professional to have a baby, another to learn to nurse it, another to take care of it during the day, and yet another to teach it when it goes to school. It has led to a situation in which society is dominated not only by traditional professions like medicine but by an ever-increasing generation of new specialized and certified professions such as bereavement counseling, lactation consultants, and pet psychologists.

Although the intertwined rise of professions and the market economy has led to the virtual reality of modern caring institutions, it is important to remember that the liberal caring professions have important cultural traditions of their own. They are what moves us when we see the Norman Rockwell print of the country doctor attending the sick child at his bedside rather than having a receptionist call in a prescription from the office. The systemic forces that have distorted modern life now permeate the practice of the caring professions, too. Not only patients or clients of doctors, teachers, and lawyers complain of the disappearance of caring and compassion.[1] Practitioners also feel the costs of this formalization of their healing professions, and their disillusionment is increasingly visible. Many doctors are retiring early because they find the practice of medicine no longer personally rewarding, dictated as it is by government and insurance systems.

I recently sat next to a young physician on a plane who had idealistically gone to medical school to become a pediatrician but, when faced with these realities, specialized in radiology instead and ultimately ended up in academic radiology. Starting with a desire to touch and heal children, he eventually settled on a form of medicine as far away from patients and malpractice suits as he could get. He had done so, it was clear, with sadness but with realism. By his third year of medical school, he told me, was trying his best to persuade his younger sister to give up her idea of becoming a doctor.

Disaffection by caring professionals—which is not limited to the profession of medicine—is a common subject of discussion at any professional gathering. Professionals mourn the loss of the days when medicine or teaching or the law were venerable and respected pursuits. It is usual at present to practice medicine as a complex economic and systemic business but very unusual indeed to practice it as the personal enterprise it was fifty or a hundred years ago. All of the pressures of the modern world make it extremely difficult to do anything but the former. Yet it is important to recognize that some healers, like Dr. Hall, somehow, in the face of all obstacles, manage to practice the personal way. These practitioners carry on fragments of a cultural tradition in a way perhaps similar to that in which the last farmer in the Saban jungle does so. If one can develop the eyes to see them, one can pick out such healers in the same way one can pick out vestiges of hospitality offered to people with disabilities in my neighborhood.

Dr. Hall, although rare, is not alone. When the little boy who was afraid of white was in a deep crisis, I was able to refer him to a psychiatrist who has no secretary, answers his own telephone, and was willing to take on the challenge of trying to understand a person who had become so mentally disordered that most other psychiatrists would have treated him exclusively with drugs. A friend with a general medical practice in Germany also answers her own phone, makes house calls, and is more likely to make a lonely elderly person a cup of tea and give him or her a foot massage than to write a prescription. A friend who is a master acupuncturist treats me at the breakfast table while feeding the cat. My chiropractor, who lives above his office, will always see you on a Sunday if you need him. These are healers, one might say, of the old school.

I find that living a reasonable life in the modern age depends on finding such people, who are living and working as people once did. This is not limited to the healing professions. Hal, my automobile mechanic, can diagnose a carburetor problem in his little garage simply by ear and then fix it with a screwdriver adjustment. He learned this from his father, who learned it from a master mechanic in the 1930s. You do not find this kind of skill at an ordinary car dealership anymore. I depend on healers like those I mentioned, on the lawyer in his storefront office, on farmers who grow organic vegetables, on the two guys around the corner who run the little café that is our neighborhood "third place," to use Oldenburg's term. Each of these people has found a way to live and work as if the world were not completely covered with the virtual reality of systems, whether these systems be national hospital chains, shopping malls, or airports. Each keeps alive this most "fragile creation of the human," which is the culture in which we find our being.

Remnants of Healing

Caring individual professionals can, in this way, serve to sustain hospitable traditions of healing professions even in the counterproductive settings in which most must work. Sometimes, however, this situation can be found on a larger scale. Although it has grown exceedingly rare, vestiges of caring can still be found in certain caring settings like hospitals or agencies or camps. Years of working on the creation of human service agencies have taught me that the time in an organization's life in which it is focused primarily on helping its clientele is usually short. Yet just as with the clinical professions, one is happily surprised occasionally to find entire large caring organizations, always under unusually gifted leadership, that remain as vital and devoted to service as they were at the time of their founding decades before. Leadership of charitable organizations, I recall, has its own cultural tradition.

I have long been particularly fascinated by the birth of the early mental asylums and of the great "alienists" who founded them. Samuel Woodward, medical superintendent of the Worcester Hospital in the mid-1800s, would greet patients when they arrived at his institution and personally free them from their manacles and cages. He would then "escort them into the dining-room and seat them beside his family at the head table."[2] This was certainly a vestige of medieval monastic traditions of hospitality in which guests, treated as the hidden Christ, were greeted by the abbot, who washed their hands and sometimes their feet as a ritual of reception.[3]

In psychiatric hospitals today, one would have to go a long way before one could find an administrator dining with his family in the patient cafeteria or welcoming patients to his personal table. Administrators of modern institutions of all types rarely even directly encounter those served by their programs. The complexity of administration and the many levels of delegated authority make such direct contact unlikely.

Yet I have been in a hundred-bed hospital for children with disabilities, administered for decades by the same charismatic director, in which loving care and compassion were immediately evident in every act of every therapist helping handicapped children to learn to walk down a hallway. I have been to a small, noisy school in Washington, D.C., that radiates the joy of learning. I have been to a colony in Scotland where some of the most skilled therapists for people with mental retardation I have ever met live together with the people they serve—without pay—and drive the bus, patch the roof, and give tours of the village with discussions of the Latin roots of place names. I am always on the lookout for such rare places in the modern managed landscape. Here and there, such remnants of professional caring still exist.

This truth was particularly brought home to me when I went to a meeting at a YMCA camp in a rural part of Pennsylvania. I was struck by the sparkling maintenance of the place, the high quality of the food, the warmth and character of the camp. Why did this setting have such an unusual feel to it? Suddenly the second morning a big exuberant fellow bounded in, shook hands vigorously all around, and introduced himself as "Uncle Harry"—the director of the camp. Within the first few minutes he had told me his story—about how he had been born a poor child in the city, how his father had died when he was five, how his life had changed because he had been sent to this camp every summer on a scholarship, how he had blossomed under the influence of "plenty of good food, loving, caring people, and being out in beautiful nature." He had grown up and gone to work. Twenty-two years ago, as an adult, he had been sent by the YMCA to close down the now failed and dilapidated camp. "I guess I did a lousy job at my assignment," he chuckled. What Uncle Harry had done instead, guided by his personal experience, was to resurrect the place that had helped him so it could help others like him.

Uncle Harry was a consummate organizer. He had the ability to inspire everyone around him with his vision. If some dads came to a weekend camp with their kids and one was found to be the area's leading architect, he and his entire staff would be recruited to come for a weekend and donate a new architectural plan. Six volunteer carpenters were hammering away building a new cabin for campers as we spoke. When a special program for children with handicaps ran out of money to pay for the summer, Harry told the kids to come anyway—he would find the money somewhere. He did.

What particularly struck me about Uncle Harry was his little capsule biography of his life and work, told to me as if it were a spontaneous, off-the-cuff conversation. But I was certain that this was not the case. This story, Uncle Harry's personal story, was clearly *the story he told to every single person he met*—every staff member, every camper, every parent, every visitor. Uncle Harry's story was the personal and now collective myth around which his entire camp revolved and that gave the camp continually renewing life. The story took only a few moments to tell but had great power. What did it say? It caused you to picture in your mind this poor child whose father was dead and who lived in the city. You saw the little child come to the camp and heard *what made that child flourish, in exact order of importance: "plenty of good food, loving, caring people, beautiful nature."* This was what the camp was for. That myth, sung constantly by Harry in his ceaseless peregrinations around his campus, served to inform the newest kitchen assistant to make it *plenty* and to make it *good*, to be *loving* and to be *caring*. At the heart of Uncle Harry's YMCA camp lay not a mission statement but a cultural myth. That myth was a remnant of a time in which charitable enterprises served a clearer and more coherent function, in which organized charities often had an immediate meaning to communities and to the cultures in which they existed.

How different this camp was from so many other places I had seen in my career—where the administrators were trying to seek yet another government grant, convert the positions of the staff to part-time to eliminate benefits costs, buy a new computer system. In my own town of Harrisburg, the administrator of our library system was progressively dismembering the beautiful stone downtown library by sending all of the books out to the expanded branch in the suburbs near the shopping mall. Here there was no myth—the myth of the old and venerable cultural institution of the central library, where so many generations of Harrisburg citizens had sat on the floor in the children's section for story hour, where so many local businesspeople had walked over at lunchtime to look something up in the reference section, where retired folks had whiled away the mornings reading the newspapers. Now the children's librarian, the reference books, the newspaper racks were gone. Instead, the administrator could tell me the exact circulation cost of materials in each of the branches and why that cost was too high downtown. The library board focused on the lack of parking—since all of the members drove to meetings from the suburbs—although almost everybody who actually used the downtown library walked there from nearby, just as I did. Like the little library in Shin Hollow, like most cultural institutions in society set up to support and care for people, the library had run into the dominant idea of the flowchart. Like most, it had lost its cultural existence and become an economic and systemic reality.

Compared to this trend, the continuance of Uncle Harry's camp and the practice of Dr. Hall are notable. They exist, we know, only by resisting intense pressure against continuance: against cost-management plans, against government and insurance regulations, and, most of all, against the sense that things should be efficient, orderly, and well-managed machines. It is worth remembering that in all caring professions—whether medicine, teaching, or charities—professional cultural traditions and myths can be found and can give life to professional work. Here and there, one can pick out those who keep these cultural professional traditions alive. From them we can be reminded that to be a professional is not necessarily to be a functionary of a system. From the caring hand of a doctor, the word of a teacher, the mythic story of an administrator, we see that caring professions, too, can be an important part of a cultural, vernacular world in which it is a pleasure to dwell.

When I walk through the gardens of the venerable old Pennsylvania Hospital in Philadelphia, I always stop and gaze at the cornerstone of this, the first hospital founded in the United States back in 1755, a hospital established not only for citizens of the city who might be injured or ill but also for strangers who arrived broken or sick.[4] On the cornerstone, set in a pit in an obscure corner of the modern medical complex, are engraved these words of Benjamin Franklin:

IN THE YEAR OF CHRIST

MDCCLV

GEORGE THE SECOND HAPPILY REIGNING

(FOR HE SOUGHT THE HAPPINESS OF HIS PEOPLE)

PHILADELPHIA FLOURISHING

(FOR ITS INHABITANTS WERE PUBLICK SPIRITED)

THIS BUILDING

BY THE BOUNTY OF THE GOVERNMENT,

AND OF MANY PRIVATE PERSONS

WAS PIOUSLY FOUNDED

FOR THE RELIEF OF THE SICK AND MISERABLE:

MAY THE GOD OF MERCIES

BLESS THIS UNDERTAKING.

Like Uncle Harry's story, this hidden stone reminds us of what all of the modern wards and gleaming equipment and people in white coats were organized to do. For most inhabitants of those white coats and administrative suits, this purpose is increasingly forgotten. But this cannot be true for all. Some surely remember the ancient purpose of a healing enterprise that Franklin set down so well.

It is not by accident that the official seal of the hospital, reproduced in Figure 8.1, pictures the Good Samaritan turning an injured man over to an innkeeper, who stands with arms outstretched before the entrance to his inn, grapevines climbing up the wall behind him. "Take care of him, and I will repay thee," the seal says. The seal and cornerstone together point to the truth that hospitality can still be found here and there within the caring professions too if one searches long and deep enough to find these remnants still alive.

In such a search, one finds that remnants can be found in three different types of situations. First, one can find them in fragments of the vernacular world, such as those remaining in my neighborhood. Second, one can find them carried on by single individuals like Dr. Hall or in small groups of such like-minded people who work within modern institutions but whose practice is informed by a traditional connection to the past, such as those concerning the healing arts.[5] Third, one may find small settings with charismatic leaders who, for a short period, are able to maintain small-scale efforts that do not quickly become counterproductive. In es-

FIGURE 8.1   Seal of the Pennsylvania Hospital, 1754

pecially rare instances, such as Uncle Harry's camp, this spirit and vision can even be made to persist for some time.

In these ways, ancient traditions of hospitality and caring can be found to exist in the modern age both outside of and even within institutional walls. This continued existence of fragments of human culture within the surrounding virtual reality may hearten us regarding possibilities of doing something meaningful in the current situation.

nine

MAINTAINING THE FORMAL VIEW: PUBLIC POLICY, INDIVIDUAL RIGHTS, AND PROFESSIONAL TRAINING

I began this book with a story about a woman about to jump from a bridge. There were two ways, I said, of responding to her: the usual systemic approach, represented by dialing 911; and the almost forgotten informal, personal, and cultural way, represented by the rescuing act of the bus driver. I have made the case that current assumptions regarding the inevitable "rightness" of formal responses have turned out to be not only unproductive regarding real caring and hospitality, but they have also made a virtual desert of the human cultures from which caring and hospitality may actually arise.

In this I do not reject all systematized approaches to helping, as I noted in Chapter 8. Life is not a black-or-white affair. Systems have their place. If I keel over from a heart attack in my study at this moment, I fervently hope someone will call 911, and I will be very glad to see the faces of the paramedics when they arrive. The question is one of balance. In our society, the formal idea governing acts of caring and hospitality has become so pervasive that the balance is skewed to an extreme. A 911 mind-set, a flowchart mentality of caring, has drowned the landmarks of ordinary human ways of living. Despite the escalating failure of a systemic approach, well-meaning people who wish to respond to people in distress act as if systems have no limits in the good they bestow, as if there is no price to be paid for such powerful interventions, and as if alternative ways of approaching problems are unthinkable. This thinking has contributed to the dramatic mid-1990s political rejection of almost all social action to help people, a subject I take up in Chapter 10.

The ubiquity of these beliefs is floridly dramatized by the U.S. War on Drugs. Over the years, more and more programs of every type and at every level—legal, judicial, penal, rehabilitative—have been implemented and the problem has steadily gotten worse. When I was in Washington, D.C., recently, it was announced that the mayor had asked for the National Guard to be called out to try to cut down on the unbelievable number of drug-related shootings taking place daily. As this plan was announced, even *supporters* cautioned pessimistically that *only* five hundred guardsmen were unlikely to affect so massive a problem! But what else was to be done? The situation was desperate. Government was impelled to do anything it could to suppress the violent "drug culture" taking over the cities. Even if few believed it would work, no other response could be conceived.

Occasionally, however, a quiet voice suggests that we look at this issue in a different way. One of these was my friend Christian Marzahn. Marzahn spent years studying drug cultures all over the world throughout history. The phrase *drug culture* is currently accepted as pejorative but this, Marzahn found, may be the opposite of the truth. He pored over sociological research of licit and illicit drug use and watched the way wine is drunk in Italy, beer is drunk in the United States, and tea is taken in the Frisian Islands of the German North Sea. In these and many more societies Marzahn noticed that the consumption of drugs is always surrounded with meaningful rituals regulating their use and intake, from the ornate tea ceremonies of Japan to the way a pipe of hashish was passed in the height of the Haight-Ashbury drug culture of the 1960s. Evidence suggests that such drug cultures act as natural moderating influences over use. In drinking wine at a dinner party, for instance, it is a known cultural norm that one will drink moderately and enjoyably and to stimulate conversation, as is common in such gatherings as far back as Plato's *Symposium*. If you wish to test this theory, lift the wine bottle to your lips at such a gathering and drink greedily: See what kind of unspoken messages you receive from your culture about your deviant drug behavior.

Drug cultures form, Marzahn found, irrespective of whether the drugs are designated legal or contraband at a historical moment. Almost all drugs, including coffee, have been deemed illicit at various times. What violent enforcement efforts such as a War on Drugs actually do is *to suppress the drug culture itself,* which is *a natural and effective moderator of actual use.* When Marzahn returned to his native Germany after teaching for six months in the United States and told his fellow German university administrators that U.S. officials considered alcohol consumption to be one of the single biggest problems on college campuses, his report was greeted with disbelief. No one could imagine such a problem in Germany. Why was there such a dramatic difference between the two countries?

Marzahn explained it this way. Students in German universities live primarily off campus in rooms in the surrounding neighborhoods. The drinking age is sixteen. Students go to the local pubs and are taught to drink—are schooled in drug rituals and culture—by the older regulars, who drink socially and moderately. In the United States, where drinking is forbidden and students live in age-segregated dormitories, no opportunity exists for passing on such a drinking culture; rather, it is actively suppressed. Thus, the result is the damaging, excessive, "cultureless" consumption of alcohol that makes dorm drinking parties a breeding ground for alcohol toxicity. As unpracticed and cultureless student drinkers are injured by alcohol, suppression is made more draconian, and the problem becomes progressively worse.

In the larger society, these dynamics are observed on a broader scale. As nascent drug cultures are disrupted, users become yet more atomized individuals without mediating structures, left alone to face the terrors of modern living, hungry for drugs or anything else to fill their emptiness and longing. When caught, they become clients of a vast drug rehabilitation, incarceration, and education system, which processes them from input to recidivizing output. As drugs are suppressed, they become more portable, smuggleable, and potent: Opium leads to heroin, cocaine to crack. And the more money that is spent on the drug problem, the worse the problem becomes.[1]

The suppression of drug cultures in the name of making the world a better place to live is a public policy example of the central issue I have been talking about: the belief that there is only one way to approach something perceived as a social problem.[2] In the case of drug use, it seems possible that embracing an informal cultural approach would reduce drug problems. Yet embracing an informal approach that cherishes human cultures seems as unlikely—even as unthinkable—at this point as Samaritans picking people up from ditches rather than calling 911. Herein, I believe, lies the central problem of caring in the modern western world.

Rights and Professionalism

This persistently wrong emphasis is unwittingly maintained by two additional factors I have not yet specifically mentioned. These have to do with the modern emphasis on individual rights and with the selection, preparation, and socialization of professionals.

After years of experiencing discriminatory treatment by airlines, people with disabilities banded together and forced a series of federal governmental actions aimed at requiring air carriers to offer them the same service everybody else received. One result was that regulations were issued governing seating, including seating in emergency exit rows. Although this improved accommodations in air transportation required for people with disabilities, the Federal Aviation Administration decided that passengers seated in emergency exit rows needed to be able to do such things as open the doors, see and hear instructions for emergency evacuation, and devote their full attention to emergency tasks. This requirement eliminated people with severe visual or hearing impairments, people unable to understand English, those traveling with children, people unable to perform certain physical tasks, and some others.[3] This provision was vehemently opposed by organizations representing blind people. A spokesperson for one such organization stated bitterly that this ruling illustrated clearly that the lives of people who were blind were valued less than those of sighted people, because they didn't have an equal chance to sit where they could reach the exit first.

The organization's claim struck me as capturing the essence of a view of society—one fairly common now—that recognizes *individual* rights above all others. The aggregation of people sealed together in an airplane could be seen as a microcosm of society: a tiny island community temporarily separated from the main body. According to the spokesperson for blind people, the most important thing about this tiny airplane society was that everyone should have an equal right to save his or her life by individually scrambling for the emergency exits.

This is a highly simplistic view of the dynamics affecting a group of people in a life-threatening situation, as has been evidenced in numerous disasters. A passenger sitting in an emergency exit now has an individual right to escape, but a larger responsibility is automatically incumbent upon that person: to assist *other* passengers to leave the aircraft. What if an elderly man was sitting behind you or a young child traveling alone? Would you leave them behind as you sprinted to safety? In fact, under the norms of a culture, you would be bound by moral responsibility to help such people. *That* is what sitting in the emergency exit row means, as much as it may represent a chance to save one's own life. It is not unknown in these situations for such volunteers to sacrifice their lives helping others to safety. If something affected my ability to serve efficiently as an exit-door attendant, I would prefer to sit directly behind some college athletes or perhaps off-duty pilots in those seats. I would depend upon them to help me. In my view of the tiny community of the airplane, I would be dependent upon the help of others to save my life, and I would have a responsibility to help save theirs. Planning for the contingency of evacuations is predicated upon this characteristic of people.

In the example in Chapter 4 about the young men who stole my car, I contrasted what happened to them with what happened to a boy in another culture who stole a pair of boots. One could create a contrast with the airplane example in the same way. Let us look, for this purpose, at one aspect of the way passengers are accommodated in voyages by sailing canoes across vast stretches of the South Pacific surrounding the atoll of Puluwat. Although here one is looking at arrangements made for children rather than for people with disabilities—a different matter, surely—the way the navigator in charge approaches the problem of special support is revealing.

Boys and girls are likely to be taken on their first canoe trip to another island when they are only five, or sometimes even four years old, despite the objections of their worried mothers, so that they will early in their lives get to know and enjoy life at sea. To this end they are allowed the run of the boat, not cooped up in the little cabin except in bad weather. Thus, in addition to seeing that they are fed and their own physical needs cared for, someone must watch little children all the time. They can swim—Puluwat children can swim almost as soon as they can toddle to the water—but falling overboard can still be dangerous, especially at night. Therefore, for any child aboard there must also be two men, both relatives of the child and responsible for him. If there were only one he would spend all his time watching his charge and fail to do his share of the work with the rigging, bailing, fishing, and other seagoing chores. Nor would he be able to take a nap, even when the child slept, lest the latter wake up and fall overboard. These and other considerations frequently require a little juggling of the roster before the list of crew and passengers is firmly established, but it is usually possible to please everyone—and those who might be unhappy because they have been unceremoniously pushed aside are likely to be related as junior to the navigator who made the decision, with the result that they may not appropriately voice any public complaint.[4]

In comparing the view of the organization of blind people regarding the airplane regulation and that of the Puluwat navigator toward his canoe, one can see two opposite extremes. Vernacular Puluwat society might be a very uncomfortable place for me to live because of its *all*-encompassing emphasis on the community and its relative disinterest in individual rights. I am glad to live in a society in which so many gains have been made in the sphere of individual rights and freedoms. Yet the overwhelming emphasis on individual rights that underlies U.S. society and that gives rise to such phenomena as a person who is blind claiming his or her "right" to operate an emergency exit also has considerable costs.

The concept of an aggregation of completely autonomous individuals fighting for their individual rights is inseparable from the view of modern society as described by Robert Nisbet. As I summarized in Chapter 4, Nisbet has pointed out that when you have a situation in which all of the associational structures in a society have eroded, you end up with only masses and central government, with no mediating groups in between. Individuals must appeal directly to government for all relief. As the government enlarges its structure and sphere of dominion in response, the freedom individuals experience is necessarily reduced. The claim of the organization of blind people would be unthinkable in a society rich in mediating structures and can be made only in one in which the situation has reached the point Nisbet described. Through such processes democracies can, as Tocqueville predicted, become totalitarian. Thus, an unbalanced action for individual rights directly stimulates the growth of the bureaucracies of formal care structures to the exclusion of informal and cultural means of care.[5]

Learning a Professional View

When I entered a graduate program in counseling in the early 1970s, the instructors introduced us to the subtleties of helping others by showing a diagram of the process of counseling that looked in part like Figure 9.1.[6] Students were informed that counseling was a behavioral-systematic endeavor that must be conducted and directed in an orderly, planned way. Detailed instruction was given about how to handle interactions with clients at each step of the process toward improvement. The faculty held that anyone "with an IQ over 100" could be trained to be a successful counselor through this instruction process, no matter what his or her personality or other qualifications.

Common sense tells one, however, that counseling other people is nothing like this. When I sit down with a person who has sought my help for problems in his or her life, I must listen with all my heart and mind. This person is not merely a machine to be fixed. Healing of this nature does not follow a mechanical process; healing follows an organic process. It is tremendously complex and often full of surprises for both parties. Any experienced psychotherapist or counselor can attest to the truth of this ob-

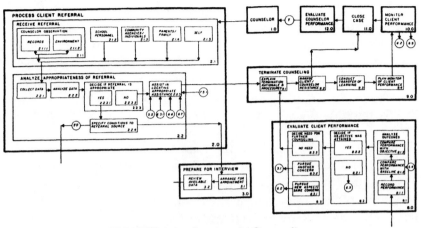

FIGURE 9.1   Systematic Counseling

servation. In fact, although careful theoretical grounding and much thoughtful experience are invaluable, nobody can draw an accurate plan for how the healing of problems in living might take place for someone else. It is a delusion to think anyone can do so.

The diagram of the counseling process in Figure 9.1 is a particularly illuminating example of how the idea of the flowchart can be absorbed as the basis for the training and socialization of caring professionals. How many "untaught" people who wished to help others were made into believers in such engineered solutions by the end of the training we experienced together? How many students with particular gifts for counseling had such gifts extinguished by their training?

Although I use this example from counseling instruction because it captures in such visible form the formal, flowchart thinking about caring, it differs from much professional preparation only in its transparency. Professional training programs based upon such a formal, structural view of the world—of which there are many—have vast influence in maintaining the certainty that care is a systemic endeavor. They generate vast numbers of graduates who go back into society "educated" into seeing formality and educated *out of* seeing informal sides of human culture. What one knows from one's common sense and cultural legacy is often erased. Graduates, in their professional dealings, educate those with whom they come in contact into this view as well.

At the same time I was being exposed to counseling theory, my wife was finishing a graduate degree in library science. In the evenings we compared notes. Striking among the parallels were the continual exhortations that both counselors and librarians were members of a *profession* and the degree of systemic quantification that seemed to accompany this claim for status as a field within the university, where "hard sciences" were at the top of the pecking order. Thus, when I used examples of the destruction of libraries as cultural entities in the name of improvement and efficiency, it is easy to trace the strength of such thinking in librarian decisionmakers to the graduate training they received in library schools.[7] As I have tried to show, the process is the same with hospitality and caring.

This is not the case with all professionals, as attested to by the exemplary professionals I spoke of in Chapter 8, nor is it true of all preparation programs. Yet it is primarily the case, which is consistent with the prevalence of this perspective in the larger society.[8]

Beginning with the way professionals are selected, many simply don't begin with an orientation toward caring. In a study of college seniors contemplating medical school, students were asked, "What satisfactions do you expect from a career in medicine?" The reply given most was *that they would have the money to travel.* Not one respondent said he or she wanted the satisfaction of helping people.[9]

Those who do have what used to be termed a "calling" to a caring field encounter a powerful socialization process such as the graduate training I mentioned. This continues as graduates encounter the equally strong socialization pressures of human service bureaucracies. Those who retain the capacity to care as professionals, as I have described, are often all the more remarkable for having passed through this process with their sense of calling and their humanity intact.

Why is the certainty that caring is produced by formal structures maintained? To understand this, it is necessary to know something of the historical origin of this belief I have explored. Further, one must also understand how that belief is expressed and maintained by an unbalanced emphasis on individual rights, by the way socialization into caring professions is carried out, and by the role of public policies—such as wars on drugs, poverty, and homelessness or countless other military-style actions—that target need.

The world is full of people who want to help others and who want to make the world a better place for those who suffer from various disadvantages. Thank God for such people! Yet under the modern conviction that care is produced by a flowchart, the work of many gifted potential helpers unwittingly ends up supporting the solidity of this social belief, with predictable, ultimately counterproductive effects. As I write, this evident counterproductivity of social systems has become a popular topic among many political figures, whose calls for radical reforms fill the newspapers. Let us next take up the proposals these politicians put forth to improve public policy.

ten

FIVE SIMPLE SOLUTIONS
THAT ARE WRONG

Thank God we're not getting all the government we're paying for.

—Truck-stop graffiti

My brother Dan is a small manufacturer. He started a refrigeration business out of the trunk of his car and now has a manufacturing plant in New York state and a new one in Tennessee. Dan and I, like many brothers, do not agree on politics. He is a strong conservative who believes Reagan and Bush were good presidents and that the current conservative leadership is doing what needs to be done. He does not speak kindly about business taxes or people on welfare. He is a vigorous member of the National Rifle Association (NRA) and writes to his congresspersons on its behalf. He proudly wears an NRA feed cap. He also has a number of guns.

A few years ago this person, whose politics would seem not to favor the vulnerable, hired a person with a disability who was sent by a local agency's supported employment program. The fellow came with a job coach, who taught him how to sweep the floor and put tools away. They were there a couple of days a week. Dan introduced me to them when I stopped by.

The next time I was in the area, Dan's employee was working without a job coach and had been promoted to full-time, with benefits. On a later visit, I found he had been moved to a workbench and was assembling high-technology refrigeration controllers. He was married and had his own apartment. Somebody else was sweeping the floor.

Then a problem developed. The man came into a tiny inheritance. It was not much money, but it was just enough to disqualify him for Medicaid, which paid for his continuing medication. Despite a busy production schedule, Dan assigned a supervisor to the problem for a day to help the man straighten it out. This was done successfully; the money for the medication wouldn't stop. Why had Dan done something so inconvenient? It was clear that my brother had developed a commitment to this man, and Dan lives up to his commitments.

As I write, many political proposals are being made by the kind of politicians my brother favors who want to reduce or eliminate support for vulnerable people in the United States. It seems possible that many of these proposals will be implemented. I believe many people will probably suffer considerably as a result of these actions. The fashion for governmental concern may be over for the present time.

What might the implications of such changes be for my brother's employee? It seems conceivable that in the future a time may come when government policies are not so kind to people with disabilities as they are currently. Medical insurance for them might be cut back or may disappear altogether. Supported work programs and job coaches may be eliminated. People with disabilities may be labeled "feeders at the public trough"— even, to use a term once applied, "useless eaters." Perhaps institutions will arise again as a supposedly cost-effective way to deal with disabled people. Maybe Dan's worker will have grown old and sick. I imagine a day when the social workers come to take this now old fellow to their institution. And I try to imagine what my brother might do. Would he call his congressperson again? Would he undertake his old employee's protection? Would he even take him in to live with him? Anything is possible—except the idea that Dan would turn his back on the man. One could have a worse protector. After all, he has all those guns.

Five False Solutions to Human Suffering

In earlier sections of this book, I pointed to many positive possibilities for helping vulnerable people in our society. Yet if there are positive signs, indications also exist of a darker side to current directions in society.

It is far from accidental that emerging political forces in the United States—the kind my brother Dan supports—have achieved success in bringing to prominence widespread dissatisfaction with governmental programs of all kinds. The political pendulum has swung once again. This dissatisfaction is especially evident regarding programs for the vulnerable. Opposition to governmental social programs, such as those that blossomed during the War on Poverty in the 1960s, is widespread for this reason. Those who wish to eliminate these programs offer varieties of five types of solutions to the problem I have identified in this book as having to do with the limits of social caring systems. The new proposals are rejecting government intervention, increasing management efficiency, promoting volunteerism, believing there is a "treatment" for troublesome people, and changing governmental program funding rapidly with a shift of emphasis to the states. Let me explore each.

Rejecting Government Intervention

In a story I told early in this book, a man saw a woman about to jump off a bridge. He picked up his telephone and dialed 911. If 911 represents the systemic approach to human suffering, then the current political critics of social programs and I agree that a "911" approach has developed into something that causes more problems than it solves. (I am not speaking literally here of the 911 emergency system, which seems to retain more functionality than most systems in the present age.) Counterproductivity is readily seen in welfare, health, and nearly every other system. (The most obvious example, prison systems, is rarely mentioned, for reasons I note later in the section Believing There Is a "Treatment" for Troublesome People.)

The solution currently most frequently proposed to the problem of systemic counterproductivity is *to turn away from the window*. If 911 no longer works, then what does one do? These critics seem to say that we should do nothing. They, like their colleagues on the opposite side of the political spectrum, fail to see the bus driver pull the woman back into the bus. Both groups, from my perspective, have been blinded to the obvious, believing government intervention can be of only one kind. If welfare doesn't work, then let the poor fend for themselves.

Increasing Management Efficiency

Wide coverage was given in the United States recently to a lamentable medical accident that occurred in a Florida hospital. During some confusion in the operating room, a surgeon amputated a man's healthy leg instead of the gangrenous one. It was every hospital patient's nightmare.

Following this incident, I watched with interest to see what corrective changes the hospital would make in its procedures. As an administrator with many years' experience, I knew damage control requirements alone would necessitate corrective action and public notice of that action. Within a few weeks I heard the answer. The hospital had instituted a new procedure. In the future, whenever a patient came into the hospital to have something removed of which he or she had two (like legs or kidneys), the hospital staff would draw a big "X" over the good part. Thus, surgeons would not remove the good organ or limb by mistake.

The hospital will no doubt work thoroughly to improve its managerial efficiency. The personnel office will change the job descriptions of the people who write the "X," the staff training department will show them how to write the "X" and how to document it, the procurement office will order the markers, and the quality review office will determine that all of these procedures are being performed as specified, in preparation for the accreditation survey.

All of these steps would, in my opinion, miss the actual cause of, and thus the proper solution for the problem of a surgeon cutting off the wrong leg. For the truth is that such an error can only occur *if the doctor does not know his or her patient.* If you know your patient, he or she is a live person to you, one who has hobbled into your office and who at last has come to you on this green-draped table.

This small example shows the same kind of solution to a problem that the implementation of "managed care" takes to the financing of health services nationally. It turns over to the forces of free-market economics and professionalism the very symptoms of counterproductivity created by those forces to begin with. As will be obvious to readers, in my perspective the term *managed care* is an oxymoron. "Managed" and "care" are phenomena from two entirely different worlds. Such terms could only be combined and not sound evidently jarring in a society erected on the certainty that care is something that can be produced.

Promoting Volunteerism

A political figure recently proposed that many social problems could be solved if people would just volunteer three hours per week. This strikes a familiar chord: Communities certainly were better places before volunteerism went into the steep decline of recent decades. When I was a child there were many more scout leaders, gray ladies and candy stripers in hospitals, and library and other volunteers than are found now. According to Robert Putnam, the number of volunteers dropped by 8 million between 1974 and 1989 alone.[1]

Exhorting volunteerism, however, confuses cause for effect. Volunteerism, as Putnam noted, is but one variety of civic participation that has gone into steep decline, a phenomenon that can be observed in social indicators from reductions in voting and church attendance to the replacement of league bowling with bowling alone. Multiple factors can be identified that contribute to a reduction in volunteer involvement: the movement of women from home into employment, increased work hours required to support a family, and the spread of television as a solitary habit. Yet there is something else as well.

In the dynamics discussed in this book, I have argued that the increasing commodification and professionalization of existence displace human culture from which many important activities arise. A more reasonable way to understand a reduction in volunteerism is as just one more example of the things people stop doing for each other when the culture in which they exist disintegrates. Are the previously claimed causal factors actually causal, or are they themselves expressions of this larger process?

An argument that an increase in the systemic character of existence at the expense of the cultural character can be made from changes in the characteristics of volunteerism itself. When I was in high school and wanted to volunteer at the local community hospital, I went to see Mrs. Fredricks, a woman everybody knew, and arranged to work in the emergency ward. Thirty years later and with a doctorate, I offered to volunteer at the hospital near where I now live. I was informed that I could not be permitted to work directly with patients because of insurance liability and union agreements. As the nonprofit voluntary sector has become more systemically dense through the process described affecting the library in Shin Hollow, such settings have become much less rewarding places to volunteer. If one is working in an intensively professionalized setting and society, the status of volunteer becomes a low one. If one has to clear insurance and background checks and similar aspects of bureaucratic functioning merely to help, the desire to give of oneself can rapidly cool.

Volunteering and mutuality are not necessarily the same. If one is a volunteer, one can be seen as giving labor to an institution, such as a hospital, library, or school. One is a nonpaid employee. This can be seen from the phrase, mentioned earlier, a conservative leader in the 1990s used in his exhortation to give *three hours*. Hours are a systemic measurement of labor. If one asked the members of the church congregation in which Nancy died how many *hours* they had given to her, the question would have no real meaning. Such mutual involvements are surely measured but not in hours, which is the language of industrial personnel offices. One sees the same thing, of course, in voluntary activities like the Girl Scouts or church groups, in which personal mutuality is still evident.

The idea of volunteerism, therefore, is not the same kind of potential catalyst to culturally generated hospitality as is asking or other approaches that have in common fostering person-to-person connections. The decline in the quality of a good life caused by the decline in the civic participation of volunteering in one's community is a symptom. To call for the symptom to be reversed does not affect the underlying process.

Believing There Is a "Treatment" for Troublesome People

When I was studying psychobiology, I read a now-famous study about crowding among rats by a researcher named John B. Calhoun. Calhoun did a rather simple thing: He crowded a bunch of otherwise reasonably behaved (for rats) rodents into far too small an enclosure and watched what happened. What took place was what he called a "behavioral sink." After a certain point, mothers started neglecting their young. Unusual sexual patterns began to emerge. Male rats even started to hang around the water bottle drinking much of the time.[2]

I am not drawing upon Calhoun's study to say that humans are rats. I am also not drawing parallels between such things as rat behavior at a drinking place and people or pointing at population density as a specific pathological agent. I am merely making the point that under disintegrating social conditions of various types, organisms of all kinds can begin to behave in ways that further disintegration and general suffering. This includes humans, who bring their own unique capacity to know and do evil.

A Hispanic baby boy is born in a large city ghetto to a crack-addicted teenage mother and an unknown father. The mother may never have known love or hope and so has neither to give to her son. He grows up in a blasted-out neighborhood in which the only remaining economies are drug dealing and social service agencies that address poverty and drug addiction. His school is surrounded with barbed wire and has metal detectors at the entrances. Eventually he grows up, becomes a drug runner, and steals a car. He is sent to Juvenile Hall and eventually to prison.

The products of this world are probably not nice people. They may even represent the worst of human cruelty and indifference. But they have almost inevitably been bred to this, as surely as a junkyard dog develops the attribute of meanness. A persistent and recurring habit in many societies, and certainly in the United States, is to label such "deviant" people as a kind of locus of social infection or even a "social cancer" to be confined or wiped out before it spreads to the rest of the population.

I have worked for many years in the field of mental retardation. Virtually all scholars in this field know that most of what we try to do today is to try to overcome the public policy set in place by our predecessors in the early years of the twentieth century, who implemented what is now termed the *eugenics movement*. The eugenics movement, or "eugenics scare," labeled people with mental retardation as a prime contributing cause of criminality and immorality. Professionals pursued missionary public education to alert the citizenry to the need for action.[3] The identification, confinement, and even sterilization of such individuals were promoted as lifesaving measures for the health and continuance of society as a whole. Thousands of people identified as mentally retarded were "put away" as a result. Despite the erection of fenced-in cities to confine individuals so identified, social problems did not diminish. It has taken many years of careful work to begin to reduce the harmful effects of this period.

Stigmatizing various groups as hidden sources of evil or even as so-called social cancers has a long history of usefulness in targeting and discharging social fears. Playing upon such anxieties has been used as a career ladder by many with political aspirations. It may be a biological aspect of societies that such "lightning rods" or scapegoats are identified in times of social uneasiness. When I was a child in the 1950s, a strange fear of Communists under the bed was widespread. It turned out that they weren't really there, but people's lives were injured and even ruined by the irrational shibboleth.

The dark space underneath the bed is currently becoming rather crowded. The present time shows a rapid escalation in the number of groups supposedly responsible for current suffering and whose removal would make life easier for those who remain. Criminals and drug abusers are the groups most frequently mentioned. But because the labeling of groups as destructive tends to spread, it is not surprising that this list has been lengthened to include families on welfare, the homeless, and immigrants fleeing political danger or economic want. The most recent nominee as I write this are children with mental disorders—some of whose parents, it is now claimed, have only trained them to "act crazy" to qualify for disability payments.

Much about this process of social discharge can be learned from examining the two principal groups mentioned. The United States now has one of the largest percentages of incarcerated citizens of any country in the world, more than even the most repressive dictatorships, and the number is still growing rapidly. This increase is occurring despite the fact that no evidence exists to show that increased imprisonment has had any effect on reducing crime.

The "corrections system" that deals with individuals labeled as criminals exhibits massive counterproductivity. As mentioned earlier, it is significant that this system is consistently omitted from the list of counterproductive institutions mentioned in current political pronouncements. To mention otherwise would be to threaten the validity of a primary social fix of the current time, that of putting criminals away. Since most people in prison are young black men, as Jerome Miller has pointed out, this fix is actually a discharge of racial fear.[4] This process is creating a vast dark basement— a "collective shadow," in Jungian terms—beneath a society in which the difference between wealth and want is growing ever greater. And as a friend once said on a personal level, "If you don't deal with your problems, they go down in the basement and lift weights."

Overlapping the criminal group is what Thomas Szasz called "the ritual persecution of drug offenders."[5] As mentioned earlier, it is possible that the suppression of drug cultures contributes largely to the drug problem while fueling a large drug treatment and incarceration industry. Drug use is unquestionably a critical social problem; the very process of identifying drug users as "demons" may be helping to make this so.

The identification of the creations of cultural dissolution as the cause of the evils thus suffered has a long history, but it does not represent a reasonable way to banish current goblins. Whether these are criminals, drug users, welfare mothers, or homeless people, those of varying political philosophies seem to share a common unstated assumption: There is a way to "treat" troublesome people so they will no longer pose an inconvenience.

What causes some people to become troublesome to others by committing criminal acts or using drugs or living on welfare? Opinions vary. Some say it is the result of an individual deficiency of character. Others believe inadequate social conditions are the cause. Those operating from the assumption of character deficiency prescribe harsh consequences for troublesome action: incarceration in prison for criminals and drug users, "boot camps" for young offenders and capital punishment for the most offensive, removal of welfare benefits for the immobile poor and placement of their children in orphanages, deportation of alien immigrants. Those operating from the assumption of social etiology favor kinder prescriptions: thousands of social treatment programs to address the same ailments and the "environmental conditions" generating them, and professional interventions for an ever-enlarging taxonomy of maladies. Although these camps disagree about the cause of troublesomeness and thus over what type of intervention to use, both apparently believe a professionally guided program—a caring machine of one type or another—will make the problem go away. Neither those who claim fault of character nor those who claim fault of environment seem to question this assumption. In failing to do so, they miss the possibility of solutions that are more immediately at hand.

Changing Government Program Funding Rapidly

A final proposal for remedying clear errors in public policy is to radically cut and redirect funding for government programs. This is not about funding per se but is about a radical reconceptualization of government's responsibilities to vulnerable people. Since the mechanism for this reconceptualization must be redirecting public dollars, changing program funding becomes the presenting issue.

An effort to radically redirect funding does make some sense. After all, most of these massive social service programs are counterproductive. And in politics, it pays to strike while the iron is hot. The question is what effects such rapid action may actually have in reality.

The error in radical and sudden redirection of funding is the problem of what may be called unintended consequences. Vast systems are so extraordinarily complex that it is very difficult to know what may actually happen when you make policy or operational changes. This uncertainty is magnified exponentially when those changes are rapid and massive.

Let me give an example. As I mentioned, because of what is now acknowledged as a clear error in past policy, people with mental retardation and mental illness were once warehoused in large state institutions. Many of those who remain there are now becoming old and frail. It is obviously imperative for government officials to try to remedy this long, undeserved incarceration and place these people back in society. This has been done successfully throughout the country. It has also been done unsuccessfully enough times to demonstrate that such relocation after so many years can be very traumatic and must be done with the most delicate and personal attention and care. Moving frail, elderly people can often result in "transfer shock," a name for something well-known in nursing homes: The move kills them. Remedying a mistaken policy by too rapid action can often be lethal in unexpected ways. Although the goal may be a good one, an unexpected consequence is the death of such people.

An important part of proposals to redirect funding calls for moving the locus of decisionmaking downward from the federal government to the states. If one wants to reduce paradoxical counterproductivity, this is undoubtedly a good idea. Ample evidence shows that the larger and more centralized a bureaucracy, the more counterproductive it tends to become.

If you are a parent of a child with a disability in my state and you have a problem—let's say you want to bring your child home from an institutional setting and can't get the money to support your son or daughter there—it is possible to gain a face-to-face appointment with the agency director who decides how county funding can be spent. He or she might be able to correct the problem. If the limitation is a result of state funds, you have to come to Harrisburg. It is considerably harder, although still possible, to obtain a remedy of an individual situation from state public officials. But if the funding problem affecting a child originates in Washington with the federal Health Care Financing Administration, it is, in my experience, hopeless to seek either individual attention or responsiveness. Merely finding a person there who might be able to make a decision involves an extensive search. As someone once quipped about bureaucracies, "A couple of *weeks?* It takes a couple of weeks to find the guy who'll tell you it takes a *year!*"

The problem with rapidly implementing a policy to move decisions and funding to the state level is twofold. First, it is prone to the hazards of unintended consequences noted earlier. Second, it fails to recognize the reasons decisions were moved to Washington in the first place. One key reason is that those seeking justice in various situations found themselves completely thwarted at the state level and thus moved, often literally, to a "higher court." Desegregation, the creation of income supports for the poor (welfare), and the right to education for handicapped children were issues that were not won through changes in state policy. They were implemented through federal changes.

Whereas the counterproductive cure of centralized control is now being recognized as possibly worse than the disease, simply going back to state's rights will predictably turn back the clock to a time in which localized injustice was endemic. To make a public policy work requires a delicate balance of free space and responsive control at the local level and certain guarantees of rights at the level of the nation. If the federal government threw out all of the choking reams of rules regarding the education of children with disabilities, it would do nothing but cause the creativity of teachers and thus the growth of children to flourish. If the *right* to education for all children were discarded as a federal law, there is no doubt that in some states such children would never be admitted to their neighborhood schools. Until a proposal for reform carefully balances and tests these competing tendencies, redirection of funds to the states is likely to do more harm than good.

The main question about radically redirecting funding remains the thoughtfulness of change. Children are taught that it is cruel to birds to place seed in a bird feeder until the middle of February and then suddenly stop doing so. Why would adults believe abrupt change may be any less harmful to people?

Conclusion

The five frequently proposed kinds of solutions offered in various forms by politicians and others that I have discussed here remind me of H. L. Mencken's observation that for any complex solution there is a simple solution—that is wrong. Imagining five simple wrong solutions does not bring one closer to conceptualizing possible useful things to do in a complex and afflicted society. In the view of history and society I have discussed in this book, I have suggested other approaches to responding to human suffering that seem more likely to be effective. In Chapter 11 I summarize some things one might *usefully* do in practice and in public policy.

eleven

BENEATH OUR FEET/UNDER OUR NOSES: SIX USEFUL WAYS TO SUPPORT HOSPITALITY

Unless one is willing to be destructive on a very large scale, one cannot do something except locally, in a small place.

—Wendell Berry

On a snowy and icy day in Washington, D.C., in 1996, the driver of an underground Metro train skidded at high speed into a parked subway car that he could clearly see in the rapidly closing distance before him. He was killed instantly. Was the driver at fault? Under pressure, recordings of communications among the driver, other drivers, and the central system controller were released to the newspapers. The transcript showed something striking.

Drivers, in the minutes before impact, were repeatedly radioing the system controllers to ask to be allowed to use their brakes—the computer was skidding the trains through stations on the icy rails. Permission was denied. Metro trains are run completely by a central computer, and drivers are not allowed to brake—only the computer can do so. Studies had showed that if the operators brake, they use up expensive brake shoes more quickly. Moments after the driver's final request to be allowed to brake or to slow the train was denied, the computer rammed him into a parked train.

The modern world, I have claimed, is composed of thousands of complex systems—systems designed not only to run trains and deliver the mail but also to educate the young, care for the sick, and help people with disabilities. Like the subway example, the limits of these systems are rapidly being reached, and many large and small catastrophes are resulting.

On the surface above the subway tunnels, Congress was in session, reacting without realizing it to this very phenomenon on a social level. The public was beginning to be aware that social systems in particular were becoming counterproductive, producing solutions that were worse than the original problems. Faith in social programs and in social institutions was being lost. In this climate, powerful efforts to dismantle the social "safety net" were vigorously underway. Dramatic government solutions of the five types I critically analyzed—and dismissed—in Chapter 10 were being proposed.

It is perhaps fitting metaphorically that a fatal crash dramatizing the problem Congress did not see occurred directly underneath its feet. It went beneath notice that in the subway and in many other systems, human eyes that see, human hearts that feel, and people who care are caught in systemic enterprises that are disconnected from human control. Although the fatal crash of a subway train is dramatic, the catastrophes spurred by ignoring what people actually know are nowhere greater than in the social and human service professions.

In this book I have criticized the limitations of current practices and dismissed as unworkable the reactive solutions of many politicians. But then, what can be done? I have attempted in my work, emulating my Uncle Erwin, the refrigeration repairman, to think carefully about what might actually be taking place before proposing or undertaking reparative actions. The parallel to a refrigerator fails a bit perhaps, because my uncle always aimed at returning what he was working on to optimal functioning. Society—and certainly the present society—is unlikely to permit such a possibility. The historical eroding processes I have outlined having proceeded to the current extent, would it not be indulging in dangerous utopianism to believe this society can be "fixed"?

Yet one must still act. But to recognize the seriousness of the situation and the futility of most reparative programs can free one in action, for one is forced to set aside the temptation to invent new systemic solutions as further delusional attempts to end human suffering by inventing the perfect machine. One is thus free to act in personal, human ways, knowing that in any situation personal and even virtuous action is still possible. Action based upon this approach is possible even for practitioners, even for public officials, even for ordinary citizens.

As someone involved in public policy and practice for some years, I have had an opportunity to experiment with actions of this nature in the field of developmental disabilities. What I came to realize in this work was that *all of the things that made the most difference in the lives of people had very little to do with the field of disability.* They instead had to do with ways of uncovering and stimulating submerged impulses of hospitality within the general culture. The effect of these experiments was often dramatic.

I have come to think of the useful approaches my colleagues and I drew upon in influencing public policy as being of six basic kinds. The first of these prepares the ground for hospitable impulses. The other five are ways of stimulating hospitality once the ground has been prepared. These kinds of actions *can* be done within the sphere of public policy and practice toward the goal of rediscovering hospitable traditions within modern U.S. society. The six kinds are:

- Slowing the destruction of human culture
- Promoting asking: Connecting strangers who are unlikely to meet
- Stimulating associational groups
- Championing "third places"
- Preserving professional healing traditions
- Cherishing place and local economy

Six Useful Actions

First Above All: Slowing the Destruction of Human Culture

In Chapter 7 I drew upon the winemaking example of a stuck fermentation to draw a parallel with human culture. I suggested that human societies generate those ways of "facing illness, suffering, and death" that Ivan Illich defined as cultures as inevitably as crushed grapes generate wine. If either process has stopped, one must first find what is suppressing the activity and try to remove it.

I have made a historical case in this book that the processes that have caused the hospitable character of cultures to be displaced by free-market economics, professionalism, and systems have been going on for a very long time. If Illich is correct, they go back as far as an inversion of the original Christian impulse of universal brotherhood in the centuries following the story of the Good Samaritan. This situation is unlikely to be reversed.

Modest space can be made, however, for the fermentation of cultural hospitality to begin again. As a former public official, I worked with some success to restrict the expansion of government regulation in an effort to spare new social efforts. This did not entail the currently fashionable trend to simply abandon government regulation to the free-market economy and the professional forces of corporations. To commence gardening organically does not mean to simply stop using chemical sprays: Resistance to plant disease must be enhanced in ecological, soil-based ways.[1] If public administrators, practitioners, and advocacy groups were to simply recognize most of their ongoing efforts at reform as actions that unwittingly sterilize the soil of human culture, that alone would do more than any other action possible. The implications of such a realization could be significant, and the opportunities could be countless.

Imagine a world in which, unnoticed by anyone, industrial pollution had caused the oxygen content in the atmosphere to drop by a couple of percentage points. What would happen? For one thing, many people would get headaches. They would be short of breath and would complain of having little energy. In response to their need, research would be funded, insurance plans modified, government programs initiated, and thousands of treatment programs set up—including clinics to treat headaches or breathlessness or lack of energy by a variety of means, from drugs to yoga. No doubt some of these things would help. The underlying cause, however, would remain undetected.

What would happen if the loss of oxygen were finally discovered? It would be imperative for the future of humanity to reverse this condition. Industrial pollution would have to be stopped. The instrument for attempting such a thing would be a public policy. If reason prevailed, governments might henceforth implement and enforce a universal rule such as this: *No industrial activity will be permitted that destroys the oxygen content of the atmosphere.*

The right of anyone to continue any industrial production would be held to this simple test. (If I am using an example that is not far from the actual situation regarding industrial pollution of the atmosphere, that fact illustrates the reluctance to recognize a problem and act to address it even when the stakes are very—even ultimately—high.) Without the constant injection of chemical pollutants, the natural biological processes of the earth would eventually cause the clear skies to return.

If much of the distress that afflicts people at this time is a result of the destruction of the cultural matrix upon which humans depend—as they do upon oxygen—to survive, what can one do? As with the example of oxygen, the solution again is not so much what one *does* as it is what one *stops* doing. Public policy might thus usefully implement a general rule: *No social activity will be permitted that destroys a vernacular cultural practice.*

Throughout this book I have given many examples of policies that have this suppressing effect on vernacular practices. If one used the conceptual X ray described in Chapter 1 to detect a flowchart mentality, what current social forms would show themselves to be institutions and systems that displace the fragile informal ways in which communities raise their young, comfort the afflicted, and bury the dead? What could one do to remove these forms?

Examination of the "environment" in which the inhabitants of the modern world attempt to dwell would reveal it as an increasingly dense virtual reality erected with the organizational chart as its icon. Here and there, though, free spaces still remain. Like wooded lots next to expanding shopping malls, these spaces are fast disappearing under the twin forces of free-market economics and professionalism. Yet thoughtful policies, like those protecting urban greenbelts or suburban agricultural lands, can recognize and slow unbridled expansion. This is true in social and human services, too.

If one could actually *stop* destroying the cultural matrix, additional possibilities for stimulating and regenerating it would increasingly bear fruit. Such regenerating stimuli, in my experience, are of five basic kinds.

Promoting Asking:
Connecting Strangers Who Are Unlikely to Meet

In Chapter 1 I told the story of Nancy, who was able to die at home with the help of members of her church. In Chapter 5 I talked about a young football player, paralyzed and in a nursing home, whom a policeman befriended. Both had been rescued from their isolation and been introduced to ordinary citizens who took up their cause by people I call *askers*. It is askers' calling to introduce people who are unlikely to meet, one of whom is in some kind of difficulty, for their mutual benefit. On the modern road, askers walk up to those walking down the street and show them the person lying in the ditch—or, in the modern world, in a nursing home—and ask them to help in personal ways.

In a world full of service systems in which everyone is very busy, it is easy to believe that few Good Samaritans remain. But asking is an activity that can be invited and stimulated. As a governmental funder, I helped encourage and support scores of askers. These people consistently demonstrated that hospitable impulses still remained *if someone would ask for them on behalf of someone else.*

The council with which I was associated gave funding to many small efforts that pursued asking in different ways. Some, called "citizen advocacy," set up small storefront operations, spent lots of time in diners getting to know their communities, and introduced people one at a time—carefully looking for the right person for each individual about whom they were concerned, introducing or matching them, and then encouraging the relationship from a distance. Others sought adoptive families for children with severe handicaps. Some drew together circles of friends around a handicapped person and his or her family.

Others introduced people to each other through more subtle and indirect means. A private high school produced a musical in which each part was acted out by pairs of students—one student from that school and one from the residential school for severely disabled children down the street. Life-changing friendships were formed, which was the real purpose of the production. An artist's colony started an art program along the same lines. There have been countless others.

I visited such an effort set up to break down the isolation of children with disabilities in one town. Over a celebratory dinner, one parent after another stood up and spoke. A mother said, "Before we met Jan Clarke [the asker] our daughter had never had anybody at a birthday party but her immediate relatives. But on her last birthday party the house was full of new friends." A father—a well-dressed lawyer—spoke next, trying with apparently uncharacteristic difficulty to remain composed. "When I used to come home from work in the evening, my son would always be waiting for me alone, as he had been alone all day. He had nobody to play with. Now when I walk down the street, I see all the bicycles of the neighborhood kids scattered over our front yard." The children—all of the children—were flourishing and their families with them. What was happening here was the result of a single asker's determination to remake the web of friendship for children in one town.

A great man named Jean Vanier once wrote:

> For the handicapped person who had felt abandoned, there is only one reality that will bring him back to life: an authentic, tender, and faithful relationship. He must discover that he is loved and important to someone. Only then will his confusion turn into peace. And to love is not to do something for someone; it is to be with him. It is to rejoice in his presence; it is to give him confidence in the value of his being.

So potent can be the action of a single individual in this way that it affects not only people in need but an entire expanding informal network of mutual support and caring. It is this simple gesture of asking that, as I mentioned in Chapter 6, was responsible for saving those Jews taken in by "rescuers," at the risk of their own lives, during the Holocaust: Most of those who extended their care did so because they were originally *asked* by informal intermediaries. Rescuers themselves were distinguished by the extent of their networks of informal relationships.[2]

Although it can easily be assumed that there are no longer potential Samaritans in society and no people with the calling of asking to bring them together, in fact my experience made it clear to me that a multitude of both exists in most places. What was required to bring this reality to visibility was to identify, encourage, and support askers *who were invariably already there.* The results were sometimes as disproportionate as the effect of dropping a little bit of yeast into a vat of grapes. It took very small amounts of money to support these askers in their catalytic work. And then things often started to bubble on their own.

Stimulating Associational Groups

Individuals—and individual relationships—do not exist independent of their associational settings. For them to thrive they must be part of larger groups, or what I earlier termed mediating structures. The displacement of such groups—what one might think of as the basic organs of culture—has precipitated a modern fever-rise in a yearning for community. Stimulating cultural approaches to hospitable caring must thus necessarily involve careful attention to such groups.

For associational groups to exist, they must have work to do. The town council, for example, cannot work to decide which ill elderly people in their town to help if all such persons are in national-chain nursing homes paid for by Medicaid directly from Washington. Without any work to do, there come to be no active town councils, no church organizations to visit the sick, no charitable organizations to feed the hungry. The organs of hospitality wither. As noted earlier, careful and balanced restoration of decisionmaking to the most local level possible can slow the current suppression of associational activity and thus help mediating structures of all kinds to flourish. But more direct actions can be taken as well.

Stimulus can be given to associational life by public policy that actively calls upon citizens to solve problems. My own former organization, for instance, a state Developmental Disabilities Council, gave out scores of one-time $10,000 grants to support the formation of grassroots citizen groups that came together to improve life for people with disabilities in some way. To some degree, *it was relatively unimportant to me what problem these groups organized to address:* making the sidewalks accessible, making the schools better, or giving tired parents some relief. The important thing was that an increasing number of associational groups were called into existence. We funded them to "accomplish" something because groups of people always come together to accomplish something *external* to themselves. We only funded them once to help keep them from the temptation of turning themselves into systems, dependent on money from an outside system.

In helping to stimulate the vitality of associational groups, one quickly finds it difficult to differentiate this from the practice of asking. When a successful asker makes a match of two people, the friendship quickly expands into larger family and associational groups in which the two individuals find their home. Similarly, when mediating structures thrive, many opportunities exist for friendship and the building of a common culture. This situation can present keen opportunities for those who wish to help people who are disadvantaged or perhaps disabled.

An imaginative mother of a young adult son with a disability in the Northwest, for instance, was troubled by the social isolation of her son and his single, similarly disabled friend. Instead of pursuing a special recreation program, she simply looked around her. She lived in a neighborhood with a very active neighborhood association. The association's newest project was to restore the stream that ran through the extensive neighborhood park. Clearly seeing the associational opportunity, the mother launched an effort to include these two men as part of the community crews restoring the stream. She got a tiny grant to help support her work. The evening before she was to have a kick-off meeting for her project, she gave me a call. "I'm about to have this meeting, David," she told me, "but now that it's tomorrow I realize that I have no idea what to try to do at it."

"Why are you having such a meeting?" I asked.

"Because we said we would have it in our grant application," she quickly responded.

"Let me put it this way," I reflected. "If you had a niece who came to stay with you for the summer who didn't know any teenagers in town, would you hold a meeting of all the teenagers in the neighborhood to solve the problem of her isolation? Of course not. You might lead a trip to the lake or have a cookout or even get people together for a workday on your stream. You wouldn't say anything about her 'problem' at all—you'd just say, 'Hey, you, why don't you pick up that picnic basket. Could the two of you get that cooler together?' (You'd pick two people for this task who you hoped might discover the opportunity for a conversation this way.) 'Maybe the rest of you would bring along the rakes and shovels.' You would know that to successfully bring people together you would have to carefully not say anything about relationships or the problem on your mind but to *keep everybody focused on a common enterprise outside of the group.*"

This woman had known exactly what to do before she got the grant. She was very involved in her neighborhood and her community, and she knew how communities worked. It was revealing that only when she came in contact with a human services field did she forget—although only momentarily, fortunately—all she knew about people and how they work. Once she remembered, she knew more than I did.

Championing "Third Places"

I have proposed that one useful thing to do in the present age is to connect individuals in mutuality through asking. Another is to promote the vitality of the associational structures in which such relationships occur. A third potential action is to champion the importance of the physical and social locations in which convivial associations can form. This has been persuasively pointed out by Ray Oldenburg, whose work was mentioned in Chapter 7.

"Experiences occur in places conducive to them, or they do not occur at all," Oldenburg wrote. "When certain places disappear, certain experiences also disappear."[3] If a society is left with only home (Oldenburg's "first place") and work (his second), there are very few places for what I term culture to form. Such societies are missing the kind of "beehive foundation sheet" proposed by the inventors of the Pioneer Health Centre in Peckham, which I introduced in Chapter 1 and discussed in greater detail in Chapter 7.

Many small things and one large thing can be done to make neighborhoods more supportive of human culture. On a tiny level, my former organization gave grants to certain associational efforts identified with a place. One innovative group concerned about the isolation of children with mental disorders, who had many doctors but no friends, built a clubhouse as a "third-place" hangout for a group of children with and without disabilities who called themselves the "Voyagers," presumably because they took a lot of trips together. A Filipino theater group in Washington state decided to renovate its theater together and thought of including some people with disabilities as fellow members. Two friends in Connecticut "dropped out" of the disability service field and started a hospitable third-place corner post office and card store instead. There are many more examples.

Planners, of course, can affect this development on an even greater level. It is heartening to see new attention coming to the importance of city parks, of mixed-use neighborhoods, of new approaches to planned neighborhoods and communities such as "cohousing,"[4] and of other architectural supports to a hospitable civic life. But if I could take only one governmental action to increase "care" in U.S. society, I would agree with Oldenburg that the single most influential thing that could be done would be to eliminate residential zoning that keeps third places out of residential neighborhoods.[5]

Because third places tend to be small businesses, they thrive wherever they can become part of a local economy. To stimulate them, only a removal of current suppressants is necessary. The primary suppressant of the general existence of such places, Oldenburg has pointed out, is restrictive zoning prohibiting them in residential areas. Get rid of this rule's stifling effect, and even the most sterile suburbs would soon have corner taverns and beauty parlors and diners "where everybody knows your name." As a bonus, Oldenburg pointed out, you would also reduce drunk driving, a problem peculiar to societies that do not have bars within walking distance of where people live.[6]

Preserving Professional Healing Traditions

Even if one holds that most babies should be born at home with the help of midwives, it is surely good to be able to find a Dr. Hall—the subject of Chapter 8—to do a high-risk cesarean delivery in the middle of the night with all of the caring and compassion the best of the medical tradition can inspire. Yet it is becoming harder and harder for practitioners like Dr. Hall, in all caring fields, to be able to practice as they think and know best.

I pointed out the seeming paradox in the reality that just as systemic caring professions are progressively displacing vernacular ways of care, traditional, personal, and professional care is becoming harder and harder to find. Thus, another useful thing to do at the present time is to not only limit inappropriate use of professional solutions to human problems but to also work to *preserve* the traditions of professional care where such an approach is clearly appropriate.

How does one judge when professional healing is appropriate? I have come to think that a "virtuous practice" of professional healing must:

1. Be integral to the culture of a particular place and not be displaced by professionalism or economics
2. Pursue intervention with the hand of a "reluctant surgeon"
3. Constantly ask if it is stimulating native healing capabilities or replacing them
4. Actually help.[7]

There is nothing wrong with, and much good about, competent psychotherapy, for instance. It is, in my experience, the only effective way to treat some people's serious and seemingly intractable suffering. It is only an unbalanced emphasis that prescribes clinical "talk therapy" for *all* human problems that can violate the principles outlined here by displacing more immediate cultural ways of dealing with difficulties. If one of a hundred problems actually merits a clinical psychotherapeutic approach, it is not very useful if the one person who actually *knows* how to use such an approach is seeing thirty patients a day for prescription appointments or is allowed only six sessions with each client under a managed care or insurance scheme. If current social trends continue, U.S. society will offer solely professional and systemic solutions for every problem, but they will not be very good ones. Support of the continuation of traditions of caring professional practice thus suggests itself as another useful thing to do right now.

Cherishing Place and Local Economy

Wendell Berry related having attended a conference on community with an Amish friend named David. When asked what community meant to him, David simply said "that when he and his son were plowing in the spring, he could look around him and see seventeen teams at work on the neighboring farms. He knew those teams and the men driving them, and he knew that if he were hurt or sick, those men and those teams would be at work on his farm." Berry called his friend's reply "a practical description of a spiritual condition." "With the Amish," he went on to explain, "economy is not merely a function of community; the community and the economy are virtually the same."[8]

When I take the train to Philadelphia, the tracks pass through long Amish fields; in the spring the other passengers and I traveling between two cities can look out through the glass and see precisely the kind of scene Wendell Berry's friend David described. Yet we see it with crucially different eyes. To us, the quaintly garbed farmers with their straw hats and hard-working horses represent a glimpse of an antiquarian age. We have no relationship to them. One might speak of the relationship they have with each other and we do not as "community," but I think Berry is far more accurate in calling it an economy.

To inhabitants of the modern world speeding through these fields, the word *economy* has a strange sound. Isn't an economy about money and the gross national product and the stock market—the province of economists? In Chapter 3 I briefly discussed the work of Karl Polanyi, who pointed out that the original idea of economies—of which there were many types—has been almost completely displaced by the single idea of an economy as a free-market one. This idea, which has spread like an infection, has reduced the ecological economic relationship of people in a particular place to that of currency. This is what divides the modern world from that of the Amish; it is not the mere use of horses or black clothes or straw hats. *That* is why they have community.

In the preceding section on third places I took up Oldenburg's suggestion that little stores and bars and cafés should be allowed to spring up in what are now exclusively zoned residential neighborhoods. But then I had to add a footnote. I had to point out that this meant allowing small, resident-owned and -run businesses, not fast-food chains. One could envision what would happen if one simply relaxed zoning without such limits: You'd find a Kentucky Fried Chicken right next door, with blazing lights, parking lots, and cars roaring in and out most of the night. This would not be a local economy—it would be an invasion of a neighborhood by a free-market economy to which a particular place means nothing. Some might object that one could not hold out the latter while permitting the former. This is how pervasive the conviction that an economy is synonymous with a free-market economy has become. But the other economy—the economy of a people's relationship to each other, to the work they do together beyond the simple exchange of commodities—does not operate in the same way. Regarding *this* economy, Berry has said that it "cannot prey on the community because it is not alienated from the community; it *is* the community."[9]

Readers interested in this issue of local economy are encouraged to read Wendell Berry's beautiful and incisive essays and stories. Let me say only that when one thinks of local economy, one is speaking of a particular place; a particular soil; a particular way of facing illness, suffering, and death intrinsic to that place; a particular culture with particular hospitable traditions. These are all aspects of the same thing.

To try to restimulate hospitality in a place, then, one must be keenly attentive to the vitality of local economies. Modern communities are not economic ones in this old sense, as Amish communities are. Modern communities are fragments of such true economy. That is why if one wishes to stimulate care, one must become involved in the real work of a place. In social services, there are organizations that counter all of the trends by donating money to their towns despite their tax-free status and others that are so attentive to the integrity of neighborhood economy that they hire staff only from within the postal zip codes in which the staff will work. These are gestures in the direction I am talking about. But an understanding of the cultural origin of care must involve seeing and respecting local place and economies in every action of daily life.

Opposition to Possible Actions

In the preceding sections I have described one overriding factor and five kinds of activities that, from my experience, are helpful in nurturing the growth of hospitable care. Having done this, I would like to emphasize two cautions. First, will these activities fix the problem and make the world a good place? Let me answer this clearly: No. Even if such a thing were ever conceivable in this imperfect universe, problems have really progressed very far. Will recycling end global pollution? Don't be silly! Is recycling still a good thing to do? Yes. Second, are the actions I recommend comprehensive? Again, the answer is no. They are only useful things to do, things I have found to work. There are others.

If what we should do is both beneath our feet and nonpolitical, why isn't it seized upon? The primary answer to this is the certainty I have discussed in this book—that care is produced by systems. Blinded by this certitude, what is literally beneath our feet cannot be seen. A secondary answer is that such a view opposes the interests of many professionals—their prestige and their money. An enormous investment exists in the illusion of the caring machine. This illusion, I have argued, has now become embedded in the general worldview. If it is illegal to bury one's dead, that is the case because it deprives the funeral industry of the economic harvest that results from burial. But no one today thinks burying one's own dead is something a reasonable society should permit and encourage. If a dramatic solution to the problem of drug use were to be discovered tomorrow, entire professions would vanish overnight; countless people would lose their jobs. A significant segment of the service economy would bottom out. The gross national product of the nation might suffer. This is not to say that people who perform this work are less than dedicated or are lacking in altruism. These dynamics operate far outside awareness and are maintained there by momentum, superstition, and denial—sometimes masquerading as reason.

Is the situation thus hopeless? Despite the powerful dynamics opposing a course of action along the lines I have suggested, one can never really tell what possibilities may actually occur in this life. History is full of astonishing surprises. Who could have conceived of the breakup of the Soviet Union? Perhaps it is worth considering, then, one further question. If some miracle occurred to make such a change in public policy possible, what predictable hazards might be encountered in trying to achieve such change?

Hazards in Implementation

Setting out to enhance the hospitable aspects of a culture does not mean one must adopt a romantic view of society. In fact, adopting a romantic view would lead one to make serious errors regarding the question of balance.

The first aspect of such enhancement might lead some to propose, as I noted in Chapter 10, that systems and indeed funding to address the situation of vulnerable people are unnecessary. Nothing could be further from the truth. Our society is characterized by a completely unbalanced relationship between the formal and the informal. During a recent presidential initiative to spotlight "a thousand points of light" in volunteer citizen efforts, my friend Lucy Hackney commented wryly, "If you want a thousand points of light, you have to have some electricity." If there had been no supported program and job coach to initiate a relationship between my brother and a new employee with a disability, how would they ever have met?

A second hazard might be the conclusion that since I note the connection between an unbridled view of individual rights as the greatest good and the growth of restrictive systems, efforts to assure individual rights should be abandoned. Again, this is incorrect. As I have pointed out, there must always be a balance.[10]

A third type of error easily encountered in implementing the approach I have described is in conceiving of it as a "program." If one is interested in stimulating hospitality, one must know intimately, as I have mentioned, the traditions of hospitality in a particular place. These traditions will be different in a Hispanic theater group, a New England village, and a Seattle neighborhood. Implementation of a *program* attempts to reach informal ends through formal means and will not work to enlarge the sphere of informal life.

A final and complex hazard is the very difficult one of considering exactly how far cultural displacement has proceeded and how much may actually be possible to achieve. In trying to make room for hospitable balms for human suffering, one is up against enormous historical forces. Can one actually re-create some of the aspects of vernacular existence, which was invariably based upon a specific place, a particular piece of soil? Or must one be content with trying to sustain something a bit different? To attempt to answer what becomes an unavoidably personal question, I return again to my own neighborhood.

twelve

WHAT CAN ONE PERSON DO?

There are a thousand hacking at the branches of evil to one who is striking at the root, and it may be that he who bestows the largest amount of time and money on the needy is doing the most by his mode of life to produce that misery which he strives in vain to relieve.

—Thoreau, *Walden*

Small amounts are attainable,
Large amounts are confusing.
Subtly arrange the outcome and nothing more;
Do not use force.

—Lao Tzu

The singing lady has sung her way down my street, the cathedral bells have rung, and the children have pushed their noisy way into the little school across the alley. I sit at the café, sipping coffee and watching the morning activity of the neighborhood. On the sidewalks in front of me, my neighbors play out their daily joys and sufferings, as do I. Here they meet, fall in love, have children, engage in bitter divorces, drink too much, starve themselves with worry, get sick, die, and are mourned. When my neighbor collapses at the café counter the owners' first call is to the ambulance, the second to his best friend, who comes racing down the street pulling his shirt on while the sirens are still in the distance.

As I watch my neighbors going about their business I see not only some of their more apparent afflictions and wounds but also their capacity to care for, even heal, each other. Through this subtle daily scene pass many people of influence. Legislators, aides, officials, and bureaucrats make their hurried ways to the capitol two blocks down the street; they dash in early for a large black coffee in styrofoam to go with fresh copies of three morning dailies and rush off toward their offices. Although we share the same street, I suspect they do not see the street I am watching, drinking from my old cup kept behind the counter.

I was a public official too. Yet in my idea of public policy the world is not made up of masses of people who need organized care or—as is the current political fashion—who deserve abandonment but of innumerable streets like this. It is here that the activity of caring takes place, in the cultural matrix of a particular place and particular people. This activity is not revealed in the statistics in the three morning newspapers. My aim in public policy was to support those conditions in which caring can flourish. Understanding that work, one must always end up in a particular place, as I end up in mine.

Long before the advent of modern drugs and antibiotics, vernacular herbal healers conceived of the world as having been created so that it contained not only afflictions but also remedies in the form of plants scattered by a Creator throughout its dooryards, woods, and fields. These plants were not "medical resources," as one now hears of threatened plants in the rain forest. The herbalist could walk through a wood and see healing power everywhere beneath his or her feet. These were not miracle drugs; their healing effects were more commonplace. Likewise, I see a world containing the healing potential that people can provide for each other. Viewed in this way, despite the terrible destruction of both plant and human habitats, one can find vestiges of something that can help in the most unlikely places. In a time in which the limits and costs of caring machines become daily more apparent, whether they be antibiotic-resistant bacteria bred from indiscriminate use or social services that disable ordinary ways of helping each other, it may be possible to glimpse what remains beneath one's feet.

From the perspective of the corner café, what healing potential remains? What holds promise of helping the very real people who live here? This is a practitioner's question, and I, like my father before me, carry the orientation of a practitioner. What will really help this particular person before me, these particular people? To the practitioner, social or medical theories are useful only insofar as they relieve suffering. This is what constitutes not only real practice but also real philosophy. As Epicurus wrote, "Empty is that philosopher's argument by which no human suffering is therapeutically treated. For just as there is no use in a medical art that does not cast out the sicknesses of bodies, so too there is no use in philosophy, unless it casts out the sufferings of the soul."[1] As Martha Nussbaum recently summarized in her marvelous book *The Therapy of Desire*, the goal of philosophy is simply *eudaimonia,* or "human flourishing."[2]

It might be said that in this book I have been attempting to deal with issues that are essentially philosophical. My interest is to understand under what conditions people can flourish. If, as Nussbaum interpreted, philosophy "heals human diseases, diseases produced by false beliefs,"[3] then the ideas I have discussed—as they may encourage the setting aside of false beliefs about the origin and nature of care—may be therapeutic. Is this view of things useful to those in public life who wish to improve social conditions? This is one test of whether what I have said here has validity. It has been useful to me, and perhaps it may be to others. But there is another test as well: Can these ideas prove useful in guiding the way one actually attempts to live in a place? This last question remained untested by me personally.

Leaving the Asylum

Twenty-five years after I entered the asylum, I finally found my way out. I had thought I had left it many times before by moving from the physical asylum to community services to government and related activities. But it became increasingly clear to me that wherever I went I encountered simply another twisting corridor of that same institution. Whether physical building or organization chart or flowchart, the idea of the asylum was pervasive in human and social service settings, and it had become pervasive within me. Therefore I increasingly considered whether action *outside* the asylum but engaged in practical activity around these questions was possible. I was surely not the first to wonder this.

Long ago, a book of Kurt Vonnegut's had a lasting impact on me. In *God Bless You, Mr. Rosewater,* the protagonist, Eliot Rosewater, does a curious and seemingly inexplicable thing. As head of the distinguished Rosewater family foundation, he spends years giving grants for many charitable and artistic works. He lives a privileged life. One day something happens. He renounces it all and moves back to the grim, failing industrial town in which the family fortune was actually made. He takes a room over the firehouse. When one phone—the firehouse phone—rings, he flips the switch to sound the fire siren on the roof. When the other telephone rings, he answers simply, "Good morning. This is the Rosewater Foundation. How may we help you?"

In his new foundation, Eliot Rosewater dispensed taxi fare, aspirin, and reassurance. These seemed like practical and useful things to do. I had to agree with him.

When I was in the grantmaking business administering large and complex grants, I used to think of Eliot Rosewater and joke that if I ever started a foundation of my own, it would be like the Rosewater Foundation. One day, as surprisingly as Eliot Rosewater, I quit my important job. It seemed to me it might be good instead to try to see if I could do something useful in my own neighborhood and city. In doing this, perhaps I would learn something about the questions I had been pursuing for so many years. I resolved to see what I might find out. Perhaps the work of slowing the destruction of human culture, as Wendell Berry has claimed, had to be done locally. Would the ways of stimulating hospitable culture I had been promoting in public policy be effective at my doorstep?

Trying to Do Five Useful Things

In my postasylum existence, rather than funding *asking* I attempt to do it myself. An isolated neighbor suffering from multiple sclerosis seems about to die from malnutrition and loneliness. A few of us pull together a circle of friends to bring her dinner each night. Soon she starts to be invited to people's houses for dinner. She gains weight; the light comes back into her eyes. For the first time since she became ill, she spends an entire year without being readmitted to the hospital. She starts talking about a future. In my daily comings and goings on the streets I sometimes encounter other opportunities to quietly introduce people to each other, and sometimes this works. I am far from the only person in my neighborhood who does this, I have come to realize. There are many lonely and unconnected people in my neighborhood, like most neighborhoods, even though some of them might seem fairly busy. So ample opportunity exists to try to do something useful about this situation.

Second, I think about the vitality of *associational groups* where I live. There used to be a great number, I hear from my older neighbors. But there are still a fair number. A small group of us pull together a "friends" group to save the local library. In our common work to oppose the plans of the flowchart-minded administration, we forge many personal bonds. Out of our association comes another group: People read and discuss mysteries together. Two other members band with a historical association to try to prevent the leveling of historic buildings for parking lots. A number of people are called to do associational work in my neighborhood; I make only a minor contribution through the library group. But involvement in associational groups helps both to strengthen the groups and to expand my personal networks, which are the fields anyone interested in community and culture must cultivate.

When *Great Good Place* author Ray Oldenburg and I were touring the bars and joints of Pittsburgh one evening, he asked me a pointed question: "Do you have a third place yourself?" I had to admit that I didn't. This was the unspoken confession, I realized, of another mere theorist. "Then get one!" he shot back, pointing his finger at my chest. So I listened to him and, ignoring the inner voices telling me I didn't have time in my daily schedule, started taking coffee with the regulars at the café around the corner from my home. After a while I became a regular myself.

From my perspective on a counter stool, I began to appreciate the depth of Oldenburg's observation that such third places were the matrix around which associational life formed. A half an hour in the mornings started to change my perspective on the entire day and deepened my understanding of the nature of society. I began to see why when Jane Jacobs wrote her groundbreaking *The Death and Life of Great American Cities*,[4] which describes the world of city life invisible to planners, she made her observations not as an academic but as a mother walking two small children around the city streets. That is why she had been able to see the hidden life of neighborhoods, parks, and even ghettos the professionals were simply unable to notice.

It became clear to me that one of the most useful things I could do in the neighborhood was to *champion such third places*, particularly the modestly growing number of cafés—bringing new customers into them, holding association meetings in them, publicizing them when I could. This became one of the most pleasurable things I did—far more pleasurable than fighting for the preservation of the local library, a focal third place under threat of removal. But we held our library preservation meetings in a café too; the library prohibited meetings after hours.

As I walk about the city I look around me. Are the café tables filled on a Sunday morning with neighbors reading their newspapers? Is the sidewalk in front of the diner a thicket of parked bicycles from the bicycle club? Is the library full of noisy children attending a book group on a summer weekday morning? These things are the vital signs of a community. If they are flourishing, then individuals are flourishing too. They are also, importantly, the places in which an asker pursues his or her calling, for the asker must go where people gather. With attention to such things, I have found it is sometimes possible to "treat" someone's emotional affliction merely by stimulating resonant networks around him or her in certain ways, without the person being aware of my involvement.

Fourth, there is my professional trade, that of *psychotherapy*. The common talking between neighbors or friends is the stuff of community. But it is very specialized talk that constitutes the healing medium of the practice of psychotherapy. For although I believe attempting to gather together fragments of the ways people can care for each other is the most important way to help, for some situations and people only the most powerful professional practices have an effect. It is paradoxical in a way that I chose as my profession a form that requires the greatest amount of professional time and intensity. For in deep analytic therapy one undertakes a transformation in the very way the world is created through one's eyes, through the medium of the relationship between therapist and client and the examination of the way in which you as the therapist are created in the session. Although powerful interventions are reserved for truly appropriate instances, one is grateful indeed that they exist when nothing else will do. There are cases in which only an antibiotic or intensive psychotherapy will heal.

In pursuing this, I attempt to adhere to the four principles for the pursuit of a professional practice I proposed in Chapter 11. I try to be respectful of the culture of this place. I try to propose and pursue intervention with a reluctant hand. I try to avoid displacing healing with professional procedures. And I try to practice in the way I believe will best actually help people.

To establish such a practice in the midst of current dramatic changes in health care, which are moving in exactly the opposite direction, is a curious experience. Since psychotherapy often takes time and careful work, it is increasingly difficult under the conditions of insurance reimbursement to practice it in the form necessary to get results. So I practice without the income from insurance payments but also without the constraints of insurance company approvals. In renouncing insurance payments, the maintenance of various certifications and licensing also becomes unnecessary—a freedom my neighbor and skilled colleague in personal transformation, the hairdresser, no longer enjoys. I try to set my fees so ordinary people can afford them, because they still, after all, afford veterinarians. I donate time to a low-cost clinic as my father donated his time for all of his practicing life, as part of the medical tradition he knew and that I can try to continue. In all, my practice probably resembles that of an old small-town doctor's more than it does modern mental health practice. I hope it is a useful professional trade and that it helps to keep an important but threatened healing practice alive.

Finally, there is the very immediate issue of *local place and local economy.* Downtown Harrisburg is hardly a subsistence farming community. What is left here of culture—including the sense of place and the economy that flows from place—can be experienced only in fragments. Yet my neighbors and I are fortunate in one way. Since our downtown is not attractive to corporations that are in the business of making money, we can experience something here that has almost disappeared from American life—a main street of businesses almost all of which are run by their owners. Each is a person my young son gets to know by name, just as the children in small rural towns used to know their commercial neighbors. Each—from the hardware merchant who orders the red tricycle for my son's birthday to the Greek family at the diner to the Chinese family that lives above its restaurant to the panhandler who makes his regular post in front of the cathedral—constitutes a fixed place in the cosmology of my son's universe and of mine. It is within the financial economy of this place that we can become a part, walking easily almost anywhere we need to go, spending our money within that sphere, and earning some part of our money. More important, one can even enter vestiges of the true economy of place, which appears on no cash-register slips.

In these five ways I try to lend my own efforts to those of others who wish to make this a better place to live. When I am successful in helping to lend aid to someone, it is usually only because I have been successful in stimulating hospitable traditions that are already there waiting to be needed. The most powerful occasions of healing, I am slowly realizing, arise from helping to foster the creation of a sense of community around an individual person, knowing that the fragment of hospitable culture itself does the healing work. And as a resident of this place I know that the cumulative effect of such comings together, such rediscoveries of community, ultimately help me and those I most care about, too. Our welfare is inseparable from that of others in the community. In attending to these things, I am only helping my family and myself.

Is what I am doing unique? This is a fair question, but it is hardly so. All over my state and the world are people who know how to do this, often far better than I do. But the greatest numbers of people who used to help stoke the fires of hospitable tradition in communities are gone today, victims of the processes of economic and professional development that conceive input and output as the greatest good. I am perhaps different only in that I come to the work in an explicitly intentional way, because so few are left to do it. But I know, also from experience, that this tradition can be reawakened in those who have the gifts for it in any community.

In my years in public policy, I tried to help others begin following what they knew in their hearts. All they needed was encouragement that their impulses were valid and a tiny amount of money to enable them to follow those impulses, free of the necessity of being employed in caring machinery. As the legislative and bureaucratic offices hum with the programmatic answers to ever more terrible social problems, such friends continue to pursue their small work in small places. But even the big world is composed of innumerable small places. Is there in such small-scale hospitable work any hope for the most serious problems facing the modern world? Let us turn to this final question.

Community, Friendship, and Transcendence

Those of us concerned about caring today do not live in a vernacular world, and the modern world is not going to return to that state. Trying to address the problems of modernity by dreaming of the virtues of a time now past is not helpful in a practical way. History does not go backward. Yet much is to be learned from the contemplation of what we can reconstruct of vernacular existence, which is but another way of saying the way people actually lived for most of the history of our species. This, finally, brings me to one thing I have not mentioned but that I need to refer to before I close. That issue is transcendence and its relationship to the ground upon which we stand.

Men and women, throughout countless generations, stood upon an earth below and beneath the heavens above. The earth was not our modern Earth, that blue globe of a planet spinning in fashionable posters,[5] nor the fertilized growing medium of agribusiness but was the known soil beneath one's feet—upon which one was born, from which one gained sustenance, and into which one returned. It was a world in which it was possible, in the fullest sense, to dwell. This way of living has been almost completely lost beneath the architecture of modern virtual reality. One can find remnants of it only in the rarest of places, which remind us of the degree to which human culture and its nurturing soil were once inextricably intertwined. Wendell Berry has a beautiful line about this relationship. "A human community," he writes, "must exert a sort of centripetal force, holding local soil and local memory in place."[6]

Without a particular soil, the ultimate question is how much cultural regeneration can be attained. In my home I am not living in the twelfth century, dwelling within the sound of the bells of the village church, cultivating fields within an ox's morning journey. But I do hear bells, the bells of the cathedral next door whose dome stretches high against the skyline, making my neighborhood—where I can walk to everything—feel something of that distant past. And more important, as Ivan Illich has concluded, there is friendship, which although not soil, perhaps provides its nearest modern equivalent—a place upon which to stand. It is the soil of friendship, surely, of which this book and the experiences behind it are the personal fruit in my own life.

Without soil, then, what of the heavens above? The two, like soil and culture, are connected. "There was a time," Seymour Sarason has written, "when it was literally impossible for people to separate belief in a divinity from the sense of belonging to a geographically circumscribed community."[7] Modern existence is suffused with longing for community, as I have pointed out. Although much of this desire has become unrecognizably distorted, some of it is expressed in hospitality and caring of the most surprising and yet familiar kind. These acts and feelings point to something beyond themselves. "The wish for transcendence with a divinity," Sarason continued, "is seamlessly part of a need for community, a community that should and will outlive its members."[8] Soil, community, and transcendence are inseparable and essential aspects of human existence.

In traditional cultures—which I have termed vernacular—there is always a sense not only of community and place but also of something beyond them. Men and women in societies of past ages never walked upon the earth alone. Ancestors, gods, and spirits were always living with them, not as abstractions but as daily reality. Those who live in the modern Western world are the first people in history not to experience this reality. Psychologist C. G. Jung once wrote to a correspondent that

> A primitive tribe loses its vitality, when it is deprived of its specific religious outlook. People are no more rooted in the world and lose their orientation. They just drift. That is very much our condition, too. The need for a meaning of their lives remains unanswered, because the rational, biological goals are unable to express the rational wholeness of human life. Thus life loses its meaning.[9]

Although the world has changed, no matter how it has changed we can still find meaning in friendship with each other. A table still remains that we can sit around as my old friends sit around it with me—talking, eating, drinking wine, giving thanks for the continuing blessing of having each other in our lives, in celebrating and in mourning. Around such tables, as Illich commented, some place in the present can still be found upon which to stand. For the table, with all of its rich historical symbolism, evokes a trinity of meanings—that of the soil below providing our food and wine, of the heavens above in the blessing we evoke over this bit of an altar, and of the friendship in which we, as Plato said, see the other become more beautiful because we are together. In such friendship, and in such community as can be re-created, we can care for each other.

It is through friendship that we can learn to see not only each other but also the complex and beautiful world surrounding us. How did I learn to see the world I have described here? Much like the way I opened my eyes to be able to see trees while logging with an old woodsman friend when I was a young man, each ability to perceive the world has come through an important friendship. There are things I learned to see only through Jack Rains or Marion Hoppin, through Wolf Wolfensberger or Seymour Sarason or Bob Duggan or Ivan Illich or Lee Hoinacki or Helen and Hubert Zipperlen or my wife, Beth. The interpretations of the experiences I have described throughout this book were made possible through my friendship with these people. Therefore, it seems to me, this book is ultimately about friendship. True friendship allows one to reveal one's thoughts and to think about things differently.

For me, the seemingly very different process of psychotherapy takes its meaning from this as well. For deep psychotherapy has its effect through the therapeutically guided but ultimately deeply intimate friendship of two people. It is true that as a therapist, for the most part I listen rather than speak and refrain from sharing my own thoughts and feelings freely lest they inhibit the free creation of an image of myself by the person with whom I am working, which is the core of the analytic process. The long and personal apprenticeship in which I learned this intricate and fading craft is a phenomenon of friendship as well.

Whether in the professionally gowned therapeutic office or at the vernacular café table, one has an opportunity to see people and the world flourish and grow more beautiful. This is especially so because of their fragility and the threat all fragile things face in the modern world. Just as frogs are disappearing all over the surface of the globe, so is hospitality. But this very process makes the individual frog or act of hospitality all the more precious and worth trying to save in one's own backyard, no matter what the ultimate improbability of the survival of either might be on a global scale. In my own small place, through the remaining blessing of friendship, I can look for the beauty in the other—whether this is the beauty of an afflicted soul struggling to come alive in the quiet intensity of my office or the beauty of mutual help or even of illuminated suffering one can come to see in the daily life beneath one's feet. In such places, meaning that sustains one's existence can be encountered.

If this fragile life is to have meaning, it will find it importantly in the way we offer caring and hospitality to each other. For this, we may eventually rediscover, a plan cannot be constructed on a draftsperson's table or even on a computer screen. It can only be found, I believe, between a soil below and a heaven above, in those distinctive and fragile creations of human cultures out of which fabric of tradition and meaning a bus driver's arm may suddenly dart to save the life of a desperate woman on a bridge's edge.

NOTES

Chapter One

1. David B. Schwartz, *Crossing the River: Creating a Conceptual Revolution in Community and Disability.* Cambridge, MA: Brookline Books, 1992.

2. John McKnight, Regenerating Community. *Social Policy* (Winter 1987), pp. 54–58.

3. This comparison is somewhat flawed, in that the purpose of the foundation sheet is to make harvesting the honey easier, and the presence of the queen is by far the most important determinant in the location of the hive. Yet foundation sheets and beehives in their entirety are carefully designed to create an inviting place for honeybees, in which they will flourish and make honey for whatever ends.

4. The issue of how this view is perpetuated by the selection and preparation of caring professionals is taken up in Chapter 9.

5. As we know from many contemporary witnesses. Clifford Beers, a patient in mental hospitals shortly after 1900, was "beaten mercilessly, choked, spat upon and reviled by attendants, imprisoned for long periods in dark, dank padded cells, and forced to suffer the agony of a strait-jacket for as many as twenty-one consecutive nights. Once, after a particularly excruciating experience, he scribbled on the wall of his room this ironic inscription: 'God bless our Home, which is Hell.'" (Albert Deutsch, *The Mentally Ill in America: A History of Their Care and Treatment from Colonial Times.* New York: Columbia University Press, 1957 [1937]), p. 303. Beers's *A Mind That Found Itself: An Autobiography* (Garden City, NY: Doubleday, 1956 [1908]) helped to launch a widespread reform movement.

6. Cited in David Cayley (ed.), Part Moon Part Travelling Salesman: Conversations with Ivan Illich. *Ideas Series,* Canadian Broadcasting System, 1989, p. 11.

Chapter Two

1. Seymour Sarason has noted that one must additionally recognize what he terms *professional arrogance:* the belief that because one's intentions are unassailable and an intervention is likely to be helpful, the decision to proceed is unques-

tioned, even though one should *know* from reasonable common sense that it may indeed be harmful. This arrogance is often accompanied by a preoccupation with technology, which leads people to forget what common sense would tell them about negative effects (personal communication, 1994).

2. Ivan Illich, *Medical Nemesis: The Expropriation of Health.* New York: Random House, 1976.

3. The nature of such "total institutions" was examined particularly clearly in Erving Goffman, *Asylums: Essays on the Social Situation of Mental Patients and Other Inmates.* Garden City, NY: Doubleday, 1961.

4. Early awareness of this fact has been documented in a number of places, including Gerald Grob, *Mental Institutions in America: Social Policy to 1875.* New York: Free Press, 1973. Grob noted that "by 1875 critics could condemn the mental hospital on the grounds that it subverted rather than fostered humane values" (p. 223). One important factor in this situation, it should be noted, has been massive centralized growth in response to a desire to serve more and more people. Even Thomas Kirkbride, who published the original specifications for asylums in 1854, advised that the number of patients in one building be limited to two hundred. (Thomas Kirkbride, *On the Construction, Organization, and General Arrangements of Hospitals for the Insane.* Philadelphia: Pennsylvania Hospital for the Insane, 1854.) This limit was quickly disregarded, as hospital buildings grew to house thousands.

5. This theme is developed at some length in Illich's and McKnight's work. See particularly John McKnight, John Deere and the Bereavement Counselor, in McKnight, *The Careless Society: Community and Its Counterfeits.* New York: Basic Books, 1995. I am particularly indebted to David Cayley's interviews with Illich, in which Cayley has summarized main points. David Cayley (ed.), Part Moon Part Travelling Salesman: Conversations with Ivan Illich. *Ideas Series,* Canadian Broadcasting System, 1989.

6. Ivan Illich, Introduction, in *Tools for Conviviality.* Berkeley: Heyday Books, 1973, pp. 51–57.

7. Ibid., p. 53.

8. What led to the establishment of such institutions was in fact a complex mixture of the wish to segregate troublesome people, political pressure to create employment opportunities in rural areas, and a selfless desire to help suffering people evidenced by the founders.

9. The same assumptions later governed the creation of the nursing home industry funded by Medicare. Health system planners *assumed* that sons and daughters didn't *want* to take care of their elderly parents even if they were able to and did not believe they might well do so if offered some simple community supports. (Seymour Sarason, personal communication, 1993.)

10. One sign of this effect is the explosive growth of self-help groups of citizens as an explicit response to professional and institutional domination. Some groups, such as Alcoholics Anonymous, go so far as to bar professionals from membership in a professional capacity.

11. This is why people often volunteer that they dislike airports. When you enter as a traveler, you must follow prescribed instructions for almost every detail of your movements.

12. It should not be ignored, however, that there are always people who won't send their children to school and who teach them at home or who won't have their children inoculated for all childhood diseases. Such people are often considered deeply deviant and are even thought to be a threat to their children and the social order. A positive lesson of history is that occasionally a deviant minority—such as parents of children with mental retardation who refuse medical advice to institutionalize their children at birth and tell their families the baby died—triumphs over such institutional certainties.

Chapter Three

1. Ivan Illich, *Shadow Work*. Boston: Marion Boyars, 1981, p. 57.

2. Even Traveler's Aid Society counters, once a fixture of airports where strangers in trouble might seek help, have almost completely disappeared.

3. Karl Polanyi, *The Great Transformation: The Political and Economic Origins of Our Time*. Boston: Beacon Press, 1944.

4. David Cayley (ed.), Part Moon Part Travelling Salesman: Conversations with Ivan Illich. *Ideas Series*, Canadian Broadcasting System, 1989, p. 20.

5. Polanyi, *The Great Transformation*, p. 40.

6. I am not implying that vernacular life has *no* resistance to such ideas as the market economy, only that the power of the idea has overcome what resistance exists.

7. John McKnight, John Deere and the Bereavement Counselor, in McKnight, *The Careless Society: Community and Its Counterfeits*. New York: Basic Books, 1995.

8. Kenneth Bacon, Ailing System: Poor, Elderly Patients with No Place to Go Burden City Hospitals. *New York Times*, November 23, 1990, p. 1.

9. Cayley, Part Moon Part Travelling Salesman, p. 21.

10. The Silent Power of Amoebawords, unpublished summary, translation by Barbara Duden, undated. Pörksen's book on the subject is *Plastic Words: The Tyranny of a Modular Language*, translation by Juha Mason and David Cayley. University Park: Pennsylvania State University Press, 1995 [1988].

11. Uwe Pörksen, Scientific and Mathematical Colonization of Colloquial Language. *Rivista di Biologia/Biology Forum* 81(3) (1988), pp. 381–400.

Chapter Four

1. Anne Soukhanov, "Word Watch." *Atlantic*, 270(2) (1992), p. 104.

2. Seymour Sarason, *The Psychological Sense of Community: Prospects for a Community Psychology*. San Francisco: Jossey-Bass, 1977, p. 214.

3. Robert A. Nisbet, *The Quest for Community: A Study in the Ethics of Order and Freedom*. New York: Oxford University Press, 1953.

4. The way local political organizations were displaced by the emergence of a direct entitled relationship between city residents and the federal government is movingly portrayed in Edwin O'Connor, *The Last Hurrah*. Boston: Little, Brown, 1956.

5. Nisbet, *The Quest for Community*, p. 62.

6. Ibid., p. 177.

7. Ibid., p. 42.

8. Ibid., p. 180.

9. Alexis de Tocqueville, *Democracy in America*, Reeve translation, edited by Phillips Bradley. New York: Knopf, 1945 [1840], Vol. 2, pp. 318–319.

10. Mark Zborowski and Elizabeth Herzog, *Life Is with People: The Culture of the Shtetl*. New York: Schocken, 1973.

11. Ibid., p. 210.

12. Ibid., p. 202.

13. Ibid., p. 284.

14. Ibid., pp. 233–234.

15. Émile Durkheim's classic study *Suicide: A Study in Sociology* (New York: Free Press, 1951 [1897]) is noted in this context by Nisbet in *The Quest for Community*, p. 13.

16. Aurelia Scott, Ancient Tech. *Invention and Technology* 9(1) (Summer 1993), pp. 35–44.

Chapter Five

1. This analysis of the parable of the Good Samaritan was drawn from discussions that took place during a gathering to discuss the subject of hospitality with Ivan Illich in State College, Pennsylvania, in October 1991.

2. Ivan Illich, Hospitality. Unpublished letter, 1987, p. 14.

3. Mark Zborowski and Elizabeth Herzog, *Life Is with People: The Culture of the Shtetl*. New York: Schocken, 1973, p. 44.

4. Illich, Hospitality, p. 8.

5. Austin Coates, *Islands of the South*, cited in Paul Theroux, *The Happy Isles of Oceania*. New York: G. P. Putnam's, 1992, p. 153.

6. Illich, Hospitality, p. 17.

7. Ivan Illich, Hospitality and Pain. Unpublished lecture, 1987, p. 2.

8. Ibid., p. 3.

9. John Chrysostom, Homilies on the Acts of the Apostles, in *Migne's Patres Latini*, Vol. 60, columns 318–320. Translation by Ivan Illich.

10. Illich, Hospitality, p. 31.

11. Ibid, p. 31.

12. Ivan Illich, Toward a Post-Clerical Church. *Ellul Studies Forum* 8 (1992), p. 14.

13. David Cayley, *Ivan Illich in Conversation.* Concord, Ontario: Anansi, 1992, pp. 106–107.

14. One can see a similarity between the process through which social charisma "hardens into lasting institutions," in the analysis of Max Weber, and the movement in which people attempt to guarantee a gratuitous *charisma* (gift) through instrumental structures. See H. H. Gerth and C. Wright Mills (trans. and eds.), *Max Weber.* New York: Oxford University Press, 1946.

15. Lee Hoinacki, On Reading Ivan Illich. Unpublished essay, undated, p. 6.

Chapter Six

1. Margaret Mead, Foreword, in Mark Zborowski and Elizabeth Herzog, *Life Is with People: The Culture of the Shtetl.* New York: Schocken, 1973, p. 11.

2. Illustrations used here are redrawn from Stan Richards and Associates, *Hobo Signs: A Lament for the Most Communicative Symbolism of Them All.* Dallas: Stan Richards and Associates, 1974. Used with permission.

3. S. Oliner and P. Oliner, *The Altruistic Personality: Rescuers of Jews in Nazi Europe.* New York: Free Press, 1988.

4. Philip Hallie, *Lest Innocent Blood Be Shed: The Story of the Village of Le Chambon and How Goodness Happened There.* New York: Harper and Row, 1979.

Chapter Seven

1. Speck's friend R. D. Laing was fairly eloquent on this subject. Chief among his books on the topic is *The Divided Self: An Existential Study in Sanity and Madness.* Baltimore: Penguin Books, 1967.

2. Speck reports that he has even seen long-standing paranoia, one of the most resistant of symptoms, collapse in a single evening's network intervention. Personal communication, 1993.

3. Seymour Sarason, *The Psychological Sense of Community: Prospects for a Community Psychology.* San Francisco: Jossey-Bass, 1977.

4. Ross V. Speck and Carolyn L. Attneave, *Family Networks.* New York: Pantheon, 1973, p. 7.

5. Speck did not say that traditional psychoanalysis and psychotherapy are useless—indeed, he practiced and taught both. The issue of professional clinical practice is considered in Chapter 8.

6. See Robert L. Woodson, *A Summons to Life: Mediating Structures and the Prevention of Youth Crime.* Cambridge: Ballinger Publishing, 1981; and E. L. Cowen, Help Is Where You Find It: Four Informal Helping Groups. *American Psychologist* 37(4) (1982), pp. 385–395.

7. Bergin may well be correct that an individual "natural therapist" is involved somewhere. But his conception suffers from his having constructed a theory

based on psychotherapy, in which the single influence of the therapist is foremost. It is probably more accurate to say that informal forces of healing, in which certain individuals play a prominent part, may be at work here. A. E. Bergin and S. L. Garfield (eds.), *Handbook of Psychotherapy and Behavior Change.* New York: Wiley, 1971. Cited in Alan P. Towbin, The Confiding Relationship: A New Paradigm. *Psychotherapy: Theory, Research, and Practice.* 15(4) (Winter 1978), pp. 333–343.

8. Nils Christie, *Beyond Loneliness and Institutions.* Oslo: Norwegian University Press, 1989; and David B. Schwartz, *Crossing the River: Creating a Conceptual Revolution in Community and Disability.* Cambridge, MA: Brookline Books, 1992.

9. Innes Pearse and Lucy Crocker, *The Peckham Experiment: A Study in the Living Structure of Society.* Edinburgh: Scottish Academic Press, 1943, p. 125.

10. Ibid.

11. Ray Oldenburg, *The Great Good Place: Cafés, Coffee Shops, Community Centers, Beauty Parlors, General Stores, Bars, Hangouts, and How They Get You Through the Day.* New York: Paragon, 1989.

12. Ibid., p. 291.

13. Azubike Uzoka, The Myth of the Nuclear Family: Historical Background and Clinical Implications. *American Psychologist* 34(11) (1979), p. 1101.

14. Mead, Foreword, in Zborowski and Herzog, *Life Is with People: The Culture of the Shtetl,* p. 11.

15. John Dollard, *Criteria for the Life History, with Analyses of Six Notable Documents.* New York: Peter Smith, 1949, p. 15.

16. Ivan Illich, *Toward a History of Needs.* Berkeley: Heyday Books, 1977, p. 102.

17. John McKnight believes the word *care* now stands only for that produced by service systems, as opposed to love, which is a characteristic of people. In this book I still use the word *care* in the sense that people can affectionately look out for each other, however.

18. Illich elsewhere has defined culture as those arrangements that limit the conditions in which scarcity occurs. (David Cayley, *Ivan Illich in Conversation.* Concord, Ontario: Anansi, 1992, pp. 159–160.)

Chapter Eight

1. Seymour B. Sarason, *Caring and Compassion in Clinical Practice.* San Francisco: Jossey-Bass, 1985.

2. R. B. Caplan, *Psychiatry and the Community in Nineteenth-Century America: The Recurring Concern with the Environment in the Prevention and Treatment of Mental Illness.* New York: Basic Books, 1969, p. 100.

3. Ivan Illich, Hospitality and Pain. Unpublished lecture, 1987, p. 11.

4. Francis R. Packhard, *Some Account of the Pennsylvania Hospital from Its First Rise to the Beginning of the Year 1938.* Philadelphia: Pennsylvania Hospital/Engle Press, 1938.

5. There are those who claim that good people who work in counterproductive institutions aid, by their skills and presence, in the continuance of those institutions, but one is surely glad to encounter such people when one is in need of them. This is obviously a complex ethical issue.

Chapter Nine

1. The late Dr. Christian Marzahn, from whose unpublished work I draw, was a professor at the University of Bremen, Germany. A memorial volume in which his work is included is Christian Marzahn (ed.), *Genuss und Mässigkeit: Von Wein-Schlürfern, Coffee-Schwelgern und Toback-Schmauchern in Bremen.* Bremen, Germany: Edition Temmen, 1995. Dr. Thomas Szasz and other U.S. scholars have also written extensive critiques of current drug policy. See, for instance, Thomas Szasz, *Ceremonial Chemistry: The Ritual Persecution of Drugs, Addicts, and Pushers.* Holmes Beach, FL: Learning Publications, 1987.

2. Another example is seen in the way urban renewal and superhighways disrupted the fabric of ghetto life, resulting in an escalation of crime and many other symptoms of the destruction of culture—including rampant drug use. In the view of the planners, ghettos didn't *have* a neighborhood culture, a view that was known to be erroneous by observers at the time, such as Jane Jacobs in *The Death and Life of Great American Cities.* New York: Random House, 1961.

3. The Air Carrier Access Act of 1986, in Bonnie Tucker and Bruce Goldstein, *Legal Rights of Persons with Disabilities: An Analysis of Federal Law.* Horsham, PA: LRP Publications, 1992, 10:20–10:32.

4. Thomas Gladwin, *East Is a Big Bird: Navigation and Logic on Puluwat Atoll.* Cambridge, MA: Harvard University Press, 1970, p. 48. A better comparison in some ways, although it does not include the nice parallel of a voyage, is the way the Hutterites, a Mennonite sect, handle the requirements for special care of all of their members, without formal services. See J. W. Easton and R. J. Weil, *Culture and Mental Disorders: A Comparative Study of the Hutterites and Other Populations.* Glencoe, IL: Free Press, 1955. Cited in Wolf Wolfensberger, *The Origin and Nature of Our Institutional Models.* Syracuse, NY: Human Policy Press, 1975.

5. A reasonable solution is found in neither extreme but only in a balance between the rights to protection of both individuals and communities. Gustavo Esteva elaborated on this when he pointed out that both individual and communal power must be balanced and limited. Unbridled communal power can provoke terrible abuses, as history documents. (Interview, in David Cayley, [ed.], *The Earth Is Not an Ecosystem. Ideas Series.* Toronto: Canadian Broadcasting System,

1992.) A tension, and frequently conflict, always exists between individual and group responsibilities. Moderate shifts between these two polarities are healthy signs of a dynamic balance.

6. Norman Stewart et al., *Systematic Counseling.* Lansing: Michigan State University, College of Education, 1977.

7. Although it could be claimed that the example in Chapter 1 concerns government expansion of regulations, my experience in government has taught me that almost all such regulations originate in response to lobbying from professional groups. Again, Tocqueville predicted this reality. I examine this issue in greater detail in *Crossing the River,* chapter 10, "What Really Keeps People with Disabilities Safe in Society?"

8. A critique of the preparation of caring professionals is beyond the scope of this book. I am interested here only in the way professional training helps to maintain the strength of the formal worldview in the larger society. Readers interested in the former issue should see Seymour B. Sarason, *Caring and Compassion in Clinical Practice.* San Francisco: Jossey-Bass, 1985.

9. Seymour B. Sarason, *You Are Thinking of Teaching? Opportunities, Problems, Realities.* San Francisco: Jossey-Bass, 1993, pp. 14–15.

Chapter Ten

1. Robert D. Putnam, Bowling Alone, Revisited. *The Responsive Community* 5(2) (Spring 1995), pp. 18–33.

2. J. Calhoun, Population Density and Social Pathology. *Scientific American* 206(2) (February 1962), pp. 139–148.

3. Two examples, The Imbecile and the Epileptic Versus the Taxpayer and the Community and *The Mongol in Our Midst,* are cited in Wolf Wolfensberger, *The Origin and Nature of Our Institutional Models.* Syracuse, NY: Human Policy Press, 1975.

4. Jerome Miller, Keynote Address. Autism National Committee Conference, Washington, D.C., November 1994.

5. Thomas Szasz, *Ceremonial Chemistry: The Ritual Persecution of Drugs, Addicts, and Pushers.* New York: Doubleday, 1974.

Chapter Eleven

1. This parallel and the question of alternatives to regulation are taken up in chapter 6 of David B. Schwartz, *Crossing the River: Creating a Conceptual Revolution in Disability and Community.* Cambridge, MA: Brookline Books, 1992.

2. S. P. Oliner and P. M. Oliner, *The Altruistic Personality: Rescuers of Jews in Nazi Europe.* New York: Free Press, 1988.

3. Ray Oldenburg, *The Great Good Place: Cafés, Coffee Shops, Community Centers, Beauty Parlors, General Stores, Bars, Hangouts, and How They Get You Through the Day.* New York: Paragon, 1989.

4. Kathryn McCamant, and Charles Durrett, *Cohousing: A Contemporary Approach to Housing Ourselves.* Berkeley, CA: Habitat Press/Ten Speed Press, 1993.

5. You would have to prohibit corporately managed fast-food and other chains, of course—perhaps by permitting only resident-run mom-and-pop businesses.

6. Oldenburg, *The Great Good Place*, p. 23.

7. This list appears in a similar version in Ivan Illich, "Against Coping" Keynote Address, Qualitative Health Research Conference, Hershey, PA, 1994.

8. Wendell Berry, *Home Economics: Fourteen Essays.* San Francisco: North Point Press, 1987, p. 189.

9. Ibid.

10. Those familiar with Rudolf Steiner's idea of the "threefold social order" understand how the balance among the spheres of human activity can be seen from its perhaps most elegant perspective. A good introduction to Steiner's vast body of work is Stewart C. Easton, *Man and World in the Light of Anthroposophy.* Hudson, NY: Anthroposophic Press, 1989.

Chapter Twelve

1. Epicurus, translated by and cited in Martha Nussbaum, *The Therapy of Desire: Theory and Practice in Hellenistic Ethics.* Princeton: Princeton University Press, 1994, p. 13. I am deeply indebted to Dr. Nussbaum's work for opening up the relevance of Hellenistic philosophy to the problems I have been considering.

2. Ibid., p. 15.

3. Ibid., p. 14.

4. Jane Jacobs, *The Death and Life of Great American Cities.* New York: Random House, 1961.

5. Barbara Duden, *Disembodying Women: Perspectives on Pregnancy and the Unborn,* translated by Lee Hoinacki. Cambridge: Harvard University Press, 1993.

6. Wendell Berry, The Work of Local Culture, in *What Are People For? Essays by Wendell Berry.* San Francisco: North Point Press, 1990, p. 155.

7. Seymour B. Sarason, American Psychology and the Need for Transcendence and Community, in Sarason, *Psychoanalysis, General Custer, and the Verdicts of History.* San Francisco: Jossey-Bass, 1994, pp. 76–99.

8. Ibid., p. 12.

9. C. G. Jung, letter (1959), reprinted in the *New York Times,* November 19, 1993, p. A33.

BIBLIOGRAPHY

Bacon, Kenneth. Ailing System: Poor, Elderly Patients with No Place to Go Burden City Hospitals. *New York Times,* November 23, 1990, p. 1.

Beers, Clifford W. *A Mind That Found Itself: An Autobiography.* Garden City, NY: Doubleday, 1956 [1908].

Bellah, Robert N., Richard Madsen, William Sullivan, Ann Swidler, and Steven Tipton. *Habits of the Heart: Individualism and Commitment in American Life.* Berkeley: University of California Press, 1985.

Berger, Peter L., and Richard John Neuhaus. *To Empower People: The Role of Mediating Structures in Public Policy.* Washington, DC: American Enterprise Institute, 1977.

Bergin, A. E., and S. L. Garfield (eds.). *Handbook of Psychotherapy and Behavior Change.* New York: Wiley, 1971. Cited in Alan P. Towbin, The Confiding Relationship: A New Paradigm. *Psychotherapy: Theory, Research, and Practice* 15(4) (Winter 1978), pp. 333–343.

Berry, Wendell. *Sex, Economy, Freedom, and Community: Eight Essays.* New York: Pantheon, 1993.

Berry, Wendell. Out of Your Car, Off Your Horse: Twenty-Seven Propositions About Global Thinking and the Sustainability of Cities. *Atlantic* 2(February 1991), pp. 61–63.

Berry, Wendell. *What Are People For? Essays by Wendell Berry.* San Francisco: North Point Press, 1990.

Berry, Wendell. *Home Economics: Fourteen Essays.* San Francisco: North Point Press, 1987.

Bryant, Christopher. *The River Within.* In Susan Howatch, *Mystical Paths.* New York: Knopf, 1992.

Calhoun, J. Population Density and Social Pathology. *Scientific American* 206(2) (February 1962), pp. 139–148.

Cannon, W. B. *The Wisdom of the Body.* New York: W. W. Norton, 1963 [1932].

Caplan, R. B. *Psychiatry and the Community in Nineteenth-Century America: The Recurring Concern with the Environment in the Prevention and Treatment of Mental Illness.* New York: Basic Books, 1969.

Cayley, David. Plastic Words (An Interview with Uwe Pörksen). *Ideas Series.* Toronto: Canadian Broadcasting System, 1993.

Cayley, David. *Ivan Illich in Conversation.* Concord, Ontario: Anansi, 1992.

Cayley, David (ed.). The Earth Is Not an Ecosystem. *Ideas Series.* Toronto: Canadian Broadcasting System, 1992.

Cayley, David (ed.). The Age of Ecology. *Ideas Series.* Toronto: Canadian Broadcasting System, 1990.

Cayley, David (ed.). The Informal Economy. *Ideas Series.* Toronto: Canadian Broadcasting System, 1990.

Cayley, David (ed.). Part Moon Part Travelling Salesman: Conversations with Ivan Illich. *Ideas Series.* Toronto: Canadian Broadcasting System, 1989.

Christie, Nils. *Beyond Loneliness and Institutions.* Oslo: Norwegian University Press, 1989.

Coates, Austin. *Islands of the South.* Cited in Paul Theroux, *The Happy Isles of Oceania.* New York: G. P. Putnam's, 1992.

Connelly, Diane. *Traditional Acupuncture: The Law of the Five Elements.* Columbia, MD: Centre for Traditional Acupuncture, 1979.

Cowen, E. L. Help Is Where You Find It: Four Informal Helping Groups. *American Psychologist* 37(4) (1982), pp. 385–395.

Deutsch, Albert. *The Mentally Ill in America: A History of Their Care and Treatment from Colonial Times.* New York: Columbia University Press, 1957 [1937].

Dollard, John. *Criteria for the Life History, with Analyses of Six Notable Documents.* New York: Peter Smith, 1949.

Duden, Barbara. *Disembodying Women: Perspectives on Pregnancy and the Unborn.* Translated by Lee Hoinacki. Cambridge: Harvard University Press, 1993.

Durkheim, Émile. *Suicide: A Study in Sociology.* New York: Free Press, 1951 [1897].

Easton, J. W., and R. J. Weil. *Culture and Mental Disorders: A Comparative Study of the Hutterites and Other Populations.* Glencoe, Il: Free press, 1955.

Easton, Stewart C. *Man and World in the Light of Anthroposophy.* Hudson, NY: Anthroposophic Press, 1989.

Falbel, Aaron. Being Me and Also Us: Lessons from the Peckham Experiment. Unpublished draft, undated.

Fox, Terry. *Hobo Signs: A Compilation of Hobo Signs for Those Whom May One Day Find Them Useful.* München, Germany: Kunstram München, 1985.

Gerth, H. H., and C. Wright Mills (trans. and eds.). *Max Weber.* New York: Oxford University Press, 1946.

Gladwin, Thomas. *East Is a Big Bird: Navigation and Logic on Puluwat Atoll.* Cambridge: Harvard University Press, 1970.

Goffman, Erving. *Asylums: Essays on the Social Situation of Mental Patients and Other Inmates.* Garden City, NY: Doubleday, 1961.

Grob, Gerald. *Mental Institutions in America: Social Policy to 1875.* New York: Free Press, 1973.

Groce, Nora. *The Town Fool: An Oral History of a Mentally Retarded Individual in Small Town Society.* New York: Werner-Gren Foundation Working Papers in Anthropology, May 1986.

Hallie, Philip. *Lest Innocent Blood Be Shed: The Story of the Village of Le Chambon and How Goodness Happened There.* New York: Harper and Row, 1979.

Hoinacki, Lee. Speech and Soil. Unpublished essay, July 1992.

Hoinacki, Lee. Cut Loose from the Rhythms of the Cosmos. *Catholic Worker* 57(6) (September 1990), p. 8.

Hoinacki, Lee. Why Do You Think It's Called Capitalism? *Catholic Worker* 57(3) (May 1990).

Hoinacki, Lee. A Farmer's Reach. *Catholic Worker* 56(3) (May 1989).

Hoinacki, Lee. Memory and Gift. Unpublished essay, undated.

Hoinacki, Lee. On Reading Ivan Illich. Unpublished essay, undated.

Hoinacki, Lee, and Ivan Illich. Health. Unpublished essay, 1991.

Husemann, Friedrich, and Otto Wolff (eds.). *The Anthroposophical Approach to Medicine,* Vol. 3. Hudson, NY: Anthroposophic Press, 1989.

Hyde, Lewis. *The Gift: Imagination and the Erotic Life of Property.* New York: Vintage/Random House, 1979.

Illich, Ivan. Health as One's Own Responsibility: No, Thank You! *Ellul Studies Forum* 8 (1992), pp. 3–5.

Illich, Ivan. *In the Mirror of the Past: Lectures and Addresses 1978–1990.* New York: Marion Boyars, 1992.

Illich, Ivan. Needs. In Wolfgang Sachs (ed.), *The Development Dictionary: A Guide to Knowledge as Power.* London: Zed Books, 1992.

Illich, Ivan. Toward a Post-Clerical Church. *Ellul Studies Forum* 8 (1992), pp. 14–16.

Illich, Ivan. The Educational Enterprise in the Light of the Gospel. Address, McCormick Theological Serminary, Chicago, Illinois, November 13, 1988.

Illich, Ivan. Hospitality. Unpublished letters, 1987.

Illich, Ivan. Hospitality and Pain. Unpublished letter, 1987.

Illich, Ivan. *Gender.* Berkeley: Heyday Books, 1982.

Illich, Ivan. *Shadow Work.* Boston: Marion Boyars, 1981.

Illich, Ivan. *Toward a History of Needs.* Berkeley: Heyday Books, 1977.

Illich, Ivan. *Medical Nemesis: The Expropriation of Health.* New York: Random House, 1976.

Illich, Ivan. *Tools for Conviviality.* Berkeley: Heyday Books, 1973.

Illich, Ivan. *Deschooling Society.* New York: Harper and Row, 1970.

Illich, Ivan. *Celebration of Awareness: A Call for Institutional Revolution.* Berkeley: Heyday Books, 1969.

Illich, Ivan, Zola Irving, John McKnight, Jonathan Caplan, and Harley Shaiken. *Disabling Professions.* London: Marion Boyars, 1977.

Jacobs, Jane. *The Death and Life of Great American Cities.* New York: Random House, 1961.

Jung, C. G. Letter (1959). Reprinted in the *New York Times,* November 19, 1993, p. A33.

Juul, Kristen D. International Trends in Therapeutic Communities and Collectives. *International Journal of Special Education* (1)2 (1986), p. 193.

Kirkbride, Thomas. *On the Construction, Organization, and General Arrangements of Hospitals for the Insane*. Philadelphia: Pennsylvania Hospital for the Insane, 1854.

Laing, Ronald D. *The Divided Self: An Existential Study in Sanity and Madness*. Baltimore: Penguin Books, 1967.

Levine, Murray, and Adeline Levine. *A Social History of the Helping Services: Clinic, Court, School, and Community*. New York: Appleton-Century-Crofts, 1970.

Leviton, Richard. *Anthroposophic Medicine Today*. Hudson, NY: Anthroposophic Press, 1988.

Lissau, Rudi. *Rudolf Steiner: Life, Work, Inner Path and Social Initiatives*. Stroud, United Kingdom: Hawthorn Press, 1987.

Marzahn, Christian (ed.). *Genuss und Mässigkeit: Von Wein-Schlürfern, Coffee-Schwelgern und Toback-Schmauchern in Bremen* [Gratification and Moderation: Of Quaffing Wines, Luxuriating in Coffee, and Puffing Tobacco in Bremen]. Bremen, Germany: Edition Temmen, 1995.

McCamant, Kathryn, and Charles Durrett. *Cohousing: A Contemporary Approach to Housing Ourselves*. Berkeley, CA: Habitat Press/Ten Speed Press, 1993.

McKnight, John. John Deere and the Bereavement Counselor. In McKnight, *The Careless Society: Community and Its Counterfeits*. New York: Basic Books, 1995.

McKnight, John. Regenerating Community. *Social Policy* (Winter 1987), pp. 54–58.

McKnight, John. Social Policy and the Poor: A Nation of Clients? *Public Welfare* (Fall 1980), pp. 15–19.

McKnight, John. On Being a Citizen. Unpublished draft, undated.

Miller, Jerome. Keynote Address. Autism National Committee Conference, Washington, D.C., November 1994.

Miller, Timothy S. *The Birth of the Hospital in the Byzantine Empire*. Baltimore: Johns Hopkins University Press, 1985.

Nisbet, Robert A. *The Present Age: Progress and Anarchy in Modern America*. New York: Harper and Row, 1988.

Nisbet, Robert A. *The Degradation of the Academic Dogma: The University in America, 1945–1970*. New York: Basic Books, 1971.

Nisbet, Robert A. *The Quest for Community: A Study in the Ethics of Order and Freedom*. New York: Oxford University Press, 1953.

Nussbaum, Martha. *The Therapy of Desire: Theory and Practice in Hellenistic Ethics*. Princeton: Princeton University Press, 1994.

Nye, Robert D. *The Legacy of B. F. Skinner*. Pacific Grove, CA: Brooks/Cole, 1992.

O'Connor, Edwin. *The Last Hurrah*. Boston: Little, Brown, 1956.

Oldenburg, Ray. *The Great Good Place: Cafés, Coffee Shops, Community Centers, Beauty Parlors, General Stores, Bars, Hangouts, and How They Get You Through the Day*. New York: Paragon, 1989.

Oliner, S. P., and P. M. Oliner. *The Altruistic Personality: Rescuers of Jews in Nazi Europe*. New York: Free Press, 1988.

Packhard, Francis R. *Some Account of the Pennsylvania Hospital from Its First Rise to the Beginning of the Year 1938*. Philadelphia: Pennsylvania Hospital/Engle Press, 1938.

Pearse, Innes, and Lucy Crocker. *The Peckham Experiment: A Study in the Living Structure of Society*. Edinburgh: Scottish Academic Press, 1943.

Plato. Symposium. In J. D. Kaplan (ed.), *Dialogues of Plato* (Jowett Translation). New York: Washington Square/Pocket Books, 1950.

Polanyi, Karl. *The Great Transformation: The Political and Economic Origins of Our Time*. Boston: Beacon Press, 1944.

Pörksen, Uwe. *Plastic Words: The Tyranny of a Modular Language*. Translated by Jutta Mason and David Cayley. University Park: Pennsylvania State University Press, 1995 [1988].

Pörksen, Uwe. Scientific and Mathematical Colonization of Colloquial Language. *Rivista di Biologia/Biology Forum*. 81(3) (1988), pp. 381–400.

Pörksen, Uwe. The Silent Power of Amoebawords. Unpublished summary, translation by Barbara Duden, undated.

Putnam, Robert D. Bowling Alone, Revisited. *Responsive Community* 5(2), (Spring 1995), pp. 18–33.

Sarason, Seymour B. Some Personal Reflections on the A.P.A. Centennial. *Journal of Mind and Behavior* 14(2) (1993), pp. 95–106.

Sarason, Seymour B. *You Are Thinking of Teaching? Opportunities, Problems, Realities*. San Francisco: Jossey-Bass, 1993.

Sarason, Seymour B. American Psychology, the Need for Transcendence, and the Sense of Community. Invited Centennial Address, American Psychological Association, Washington, D.C., 1992.

Sarason, Seymour B. *Letters to a Serious Education President*. Newbury Park, CA: Corwin Press, 1992.

Sarason, Seymour B. *The Predictable Failure of Educational Reform*. San Francisco: Jossey-Bass, 1991.

Sarason, Seymour B. Taking Intractability Seriously. *Readings: A Journal of Reviews and Commentary in Mental Health* (March 1991), pp. 8–10.

Sarason, Seymour B. *The Challenge of Art to Psychology*. New Haven: Yale University Press, 1990.

Sarason, Seymour B. *Caring and Compassion in Clinical Practice*. San Francisco: Jossey-Bass, 1985.

Sarason, Seymour B., and Elizabeth Lorentz. *The Challenge of the Resource Exchange Network*. San Francisco: Jossey-Bass, 1979.

Sarason, Seymour B. The Nature of Problem Solving in Social Action. *American Psychologist* 33(4) (April 1978), pp. 370–380.

Sarason, Seymour B. An Unsuccessful War on Poverty? *American Psychologist* 33(9) (September 1978), pp. 831–839.

Sarason, Seymour B. *Human Services and Resource Networks*. San Francisco: Jossey-Bass, 1977.

Sarason, Seymour B. *The Psychological Sense of Community: Prospects for a Community Psychology.* San Francisco: Jossey-Bass, 1977.

Schrag, Peter. Ivan Illich: The Christian as Rebel. *Saturday Review,* July 19, 1969, pp. 14–19.

Schwartz, David B. *Crossing the River: Creating a Conceptual Revolution in Community and Disability.* Cambridge, MA: Brookline Books, 1992.

Schwartz, David B. An Occasion to Think About Healing: A Letter to Ivan Illich. *Journal of Traditional Acupuncture* 14(2) (1992), pp. 15–18, 49–50.

Scott, Aurelia. Ancient Tech. *Invention and Technology* 9(1) (Summer 1993), pp. 35–44.

Skinner, B. F. *Walden II.* New York: Macmillan, 1962 [1942].

Soukhanov, Anne, "Word Watch." *Atlantic* 270(2) (1992), p. 104.

Speck, Ross V., and Carolyn L. Attneave. *Family Networks.* New York: Pantheon, 1973.

Stan Richards and Associates. *Hobo Signs: A Lament for the Most Communicative Symbolism of Them All.* Dallas: Stan Richards and Associates, 1974.

Steinbeck, John, and Edward Ricketts. *Sea of Cortez: A Leisurely Journal of Travel and Research.* Mount Vernon, NY: Paul P. Appel, 1982.

Stewart, Norman R., Bob Winiborn, Richard Johnson, Herbert Burns Jr., and James Engelkes. *Systematic Counseling.* Lansing: Michigan State University, College of Education, 1977.

Sumarah, John. L'Arche: Philosophy and Ideology. *Mental Retardation* 25(3) (1987), pp. 165–169.

Szasz, Thomas. *Ceremonial Chemistry: The Ritual Persecution of Drugs, Addicts, and Pushers.* Holmes Beach, FL: Learning Publications, 1987.

Tocqueville, Alexis de. *Democracy in America* (Reeve Translation). Edited by Phillips Bradley. New York: Knopf, 1945 [1840].

Tucker, Bonnie, and Bruce Goldstein. *Legal Rights of Persons with Disabilities: An Analysis of Federal Law.* Horsham, PA: LRP Publications, 1992, 10:20–10:32.

Uzoka, Azubike. The Myth of the Nuclear Family: Historical Background and Clinical Implications. *American Psychologist* 34(11) (1979), pp. 1095–1106.

Vanier, Jean. *Community and Growth: Our Pilgrimage Together.* Toronto: Griffin House, 1979.

Vonnegut, Kurt. *God Bless You, Mr. Rosewater, or, Pearls Before Swine.* New York: Dell, 1965.

Wolfensberger, Wolf. A Personal Interpretation of the Mental Retardation Scene in Light of the Signs of the Times. Unpublished essay, 1993.

Wolfensberger, Wolf. *The Origin and Nature of Our Institutional Models.* Syracuse, NY: Human Policy Press, 1975.

Woodson, Robert L. *A Summons to Life: Mediating Structures and the Prevention of Youth Crime.* Cambridge: Ballinger Publishing, 1981.

Worsley, J. R. *Acupuncture: Is It for You?* Rockport, MA: Element, 1988.

Zborowski, Mark, and Elizabeth Herzog. *Life Is with People: The Culture of the Shtetl.* New York: Schocken, 1973.

ABOUT THE BOOK AND AUTHOR

Why have modern caring systems in social services, the medical field, and disability areas become counterproductive for so many of the people they serve? Should caring be reduced to a product of social machinery? Is it realistic to expect successful systematic reform of our institutions, or can we find hidden alternatives to our current systems?

Addressing these and other contemporary issues, David Schwartz draws on multiple and diverse sources, including the work of social philosopher Ivan Illich, to suggest we rediscover informal approaches to caring (Illich's theory of hospitality). Identifying many community-based approaches such as asking, retribalization, and the use of natural therapists, the author recommends we employ these approaches to reach those who are made invisible through existing ritual segregation systems. Evaluating our modern Western helping forms, the author notes how these have developed into a fundamental misunderstanding of the nature of care and how this misunderstanding permeates our notions of community to the neglect of culture and compassion. Schwartz makes a compelling case for returning to community-based supports, offering practical and useful alternatives for individuals and professionals that are lifted from successful endeavors in clinical and social service environments.

With a foreword by Ivan Illich and selections from his own practice, such as the account of "the little boy who was afraid of white," this provocative and stimulating book is appropriate for upper-level or graduate-level courses in clinical social work, community psychology, sociology, and the health sciences.

David B. Schwartz, Ph.D., is the former director of the Pennsylvania Developmental Disabilities Council, the author of *Crossing the River: Creating a Conceptual Revolution in Community and Disability*, and a psychotherapist in private practice.

INDEX